LANGUAGE, IDENTITY, AND STEREOTYPE AMONG SOUTHEAST ASIAN AMERICAN YOUTH

The Other Asian

LANGUAGE, IDENTITY, AND STEREOTYPE AMONG SOUTHEAST ASIAN AMERICAN YOUTH

The Other Asian

Angela Reyes
Hunter College, City University of New York

LEA

LAWRENCE ERLBAUM ASSOCIATES, PUBLISHERS

2007   Mahwah, New Jersey   London

Chapter 3 is a revised version of: Reyes, A. (2005). Appropriation of African American slang by Asian American youth. *Journal of Sociolinguistics. 9*(4), 509–532. Copyright Blackwell Publishing. Used with permission.

Chapter 4 contains a revised version of: Reyes, A. (2004). Asian American stereotypes as circulating resource. *Pragmatics, 14*(2/3), 173–192. Copyright International Pragmatics Association. Used with permission.

Chapter 5 contains a revised version of: Reyes, A. (2002). "Are you losing your culture?"; Poetics, indexicality, and Asian American identity. *Discourse Studies, 4*(2), 183–199. Copyright Sage Publications. Used with permission.

Lawrence Erlbaum Associates, Inc., Publishers
10 Industrial Avenue
Mahwah, New Jersey 07430
www.erlbaum.com

E
184
.S695
R49
2006

Cover design by Tomai Maridou

Library of Congress Cataloging-in-Publication Data

Reyes, Angela, 1970–
    Language, identity, and stereotype among Southeast Asian American youth : the other Asian / Angela Reyes.
        p. cm.
Includes bibliographical references and index.
ISBN 0-8058-5539-4 (cloth : alk. paper)
1. Southeast Asian American youth—Social conditions. 2. Southeast Asian Americans—Racial identity. 3. Southeast Asian Americans—Ethnic identity. 4. Stereotype (Psychology)—United States—Case studies. 5. Anthropological linguistic—United States—Case studies. 6. United States—Race relations. 7. United States—Ethnic relations.   I. Title.
E184.S695R49   2006
305.235089'95073—dc22   2006004214
                                                                                    CIP

Books published by Lawrence Erlbaum Associates are printed on acid-free paper, and their bindings are chosen for strength and durability.

Printed in the United States of America
10 9 8 7 6 5 4 3 2 1

For my parents and for my brother

Contents

Preface   ix

1   The Other Asian: Emergence of an Identity   1

2   "No Kiss, No Money": Constructing Identities
With Asian Newcomer Stereotypes   31

3   "Aite" and "Na Mean": Constructing Identities
With African American Stereotypes   62

4   From Storeowners to Minivan Drivers: Building Panethnicity
With Asian American Stereotypes   89

5   "Yo, Yo, He Cambo": Dismantling Panethnicity
With Asian American Stereotypes   115

6   Implications for Minority Youth in Alternative Education
and Grassroots Video   145

References   **158**

Appendix: Transcription Conventions   **171**

Author Index   **175**

Subject Index   **179**

Preface

This book explores how Southeast Asian American youth formed their identities in relation to stereotypes. Drawing on 4 years of ethnographic and discourse data at an after-school video-making project for Cambodian, Vietnamese, Laotian, and ethnic Chinese American teenagers, this study examines the multiple ways in which youth understood and used stereotypes as resources for constructing a sense of who they were. This book reveals how broad concepts, such as identity, stereotype, race, ethnicity, and culture, emerge from interaction and are more flexible and multidimensional than is commonly perceived. Considering how Asian Americans can be uniquely positioned in U.S. racial discourses as forever foreigners, honorary Whites, and problem minorities, this study investigates how the teens drew on stereotypes of speech styles to create identities that positioned them with or against images of Asian newcomers and African Americans. This book also explores how Asian American panethnicity was created or dismantled, depending on the conversational contexts within which stereotypes were used. Whereas the teens drew on stereotypes to establish a common racial identity in some situations, in other situations they rejected a panethnic Asian American identity by using stereotypes to highlight their unique experiences and identities as Southeast Asian Americans, dubbed the "Other Asians" by one participant.

There are two distinctive features that set this book apart from previous research. First, this study focuses squarely on the discourse practices of Asian Americans. Whereas African Americans and Latino Americans have received a fair amount of attention from sociolinguists, Asian Americans—particularly Southeast Asian American youth—have been relatively absent from the research literature. Second, this book explores the concept of stereotype from a linguistic anthropological perspective. Most research on stereotypes has been carried out by social psychologists. This study, however, illustrates an innovative approach by using ethnographic and discourse analytic methods to examine the controversial and slippery concept of stereotype.

CHAPTER OVERVIEW

Chapter 1 provides the theoretical and methodological framework for this study of language, identity, and stereotype among Southeast Asian American youth. After discussing historical, political, and interactional perspectives on Asian American identities and stereotypes, this chapter introduces the research setting, participants, and methods of data collection and analysis.

Chapters 2 and 3 highlight how the Southeast Asian American teenagers dealt frequently with the forever foreigner and problem minority stereotypes. Chapter 2 explores how the teens constructed identities in relation to the foreigner stereotype through the derogatory term "F.O.B." (Fresh Off the Boat), which was used to label recently arrived Asian immigrants. I investigate the multiple ways in which the teens responded to the production of English with an Asian accent—what is called Mock Asian (Chun, 2004)—in mainstream media. I also explore how the teens scripted and performed Mock Asian in their videos to produce the newcomer identity. In chapter 3, I examine how the teens established identities in relation to African American youth culture through stereotypes of African American slang. This chapter reveals how some teens used speech styles associated with African Americans to create alliances with African Americans, whereas others used these styles to position themselves or others in relation to stereotypes of African Americans as problem minorities. I also examine how the display of African American speech styles served as one way for teens to create social boundaries, not only between teens and adults but also between each other.

The next two chapters look closely at the possibilities and pitfalls of Asian American panethnicity. Chapter 4 reveals the local ways in which the teens used stereotypes to interactionally construct panethnic identities. I examine how conversations about stereotypes momentarily redrew racial and ethnic community boundaries as ethnic-specific stereotypes were widened and applied to a larger panethnic Asian American community in which the teens claimed membership. In chapter 5, I discuss the opposite process: how Asian American panethnicity was challenged through the use of stereotypes. This chapter examines the ways in which the stereotype that all Asian Americans are Chinese intersected with the lives of the Southeast Asian American teenagers. Largely resenting this stereotype, the teens argued for more ethnic recognizability by highlighting cultural distinctions between Asian ethnic groups, thus foregrounding issues of ethnic diversity at the expense of a unified Asian American panethnic identity.

In chapter 6, I discuss broader implications of this book. I first underscore the advantages of the methodological approach used in this study to examine how individuals make use of broad macrolevel concepts in situated discursive practice. This final chapter also addresses the benefits and challenges of alternative educational settings and grassroots video-making programs for minority youth. I suggest that the findings regarding this particular group of Asian American teenagers add to the understanding of the experiences and perspectives of other linguistic, racial, and immigrant minorities in other parts of the United States and in other educational and media sites.

ACKNOWLEDGMENTS

I would like to express my deep gratitude to those individuals who were invaluable in the researching and writing of this book. First, my warmest thanks to everyone at the Asian Arts Initiative, especially Gayle Isa, Huong Nghiem, Kevin Ching, Leizle Talangbayan, Monica Santos, Mimi Trinh, Gary San Angel, Shivaani Selvaraj, Alix Webb, Anita Thakkur, Lori Sasaki, Gena Heng, Phally Chroy, Cham Mann, Tien Duong, Em Ung, and Danny Sieng. I am also extremely grateful to my mentors, who provided generous feedback on earlier drafts of this manuscript. I am particularly indebted to Asif Agha for his own research and thinking that profoundly inspired the focus of this book. I also thank Stanton Wortham, whose insightful feedback on my ongoing work pushed the rigor of this study. Greatly shaping how I think and approach scholarship, Nancy H. Hornberger guided me throughout each step of the research process for this book. I thank Nancy, Stanton, and Asif for their generous support over the past several years. Many other colleagues have thoughtfully advised me throughout the book-writing process. I owe special gratitude to Mary Bucholtz, who spent countless hours closely reading earlier drafts of this manuscript, offering detailed feedback, and providing a clear direction in the revision process. I also thank Betsy Rymes, Tere Pica, Tamara Sniad, Adrienne Lo, Rebecca Freeman Field, Diana Schwinge, Rosane Rocher, Grace Kao, and Karen Su for their inspiration and encouragement. Naomi Silverman and Sarah Wright of Lawrence Erlbaum have offered keen editorial guidance. For funding support that enabled me to research and write this book, I thank the Ford Foundation, the U.S. Department of Education, the Samuel S. Fels Fund, the Bridging the Gaps Program, the George N. Shuster Fund, the Professional Staff Congress of the City University of New York, and the Graduate School of Education and Asian American Studies Program of the University of Pennsylvania. Finally, I would like to thank Sam and Anna for their love, support, and inspiration.

1

The Other Asian:
Emergence of an Identity

I feel like post-Vietnam wave of immigrant, that we really don't have the Asian American identity that's been identified [as] the Asian American experience ... We should be able to identify ourselves and categorize ourselves into the "Other Asian" ... For [Asian Americans] it's all like idealizing of the American value, of hard work and money. But then for the Other Asian, my kind came here for liberation, to liberate, to be like free as opposed to come here to see America as a prospect. We came here because it was bad in our country, and it's better here for us. So our reason to be here is to start a whole new life, but not start a whole new life and put ourselves as part of the American pie. That's how I see it. We're not here to say we want to be a part of this. We're here because we're running away from what happened. We didn't get run away, we got chased out, not even by our own people, by America itself. The whole bombing, Nixon and stuff, the bombing in Cambodia allowed Pol Pot to come in. Really though, I see it like we don't even want to be here.

—Sokla,[1] 2002

When I was casually invited by my friend Bi to volunteer at a new after-school video-making project for Southeast Asian refugee youth in Philadelphia, it felt more like I accidentally stumbled into an open, vibrant space bustling with teenagers who were scattered across a bright teal blue floor. More than a dozen young men, clad in baggy pants and loose designer shirts, dominated the room, chatting, sketching, and break dancing as hip hop music pulsed moderately in

---

[1]All names used for participants are pseudonyms.

the background. A half dozen 20-something adults were milling about, some exchanging names and laughs with the teenagers, others fumbling for flyers, markers, and other materials. A trio of young women clung together. For one activity I was assigned to join them. On a large piece of paper, the girls were asked to write about and draw pictures of themselves, providing information such as their names and where they or their families immigrated from. Ny said that although she came from Thailand, she was ethnically "mixed" Vietnamese, Lao, and Cambodian. Amy explained that she was Chinese but from Southeast Asia; she used to live in California. Kai said she was Lao but born in a refugee processing center in the Philippines. Kai used to be in a gang and told us a story about taunting prostitutes, then clambering over a fence as high heels were thrown at her and her friends. I was delighted but puzzled by how forthcoming these teenagers were with me, a complete stranger until about a half hour earlier. They seemed to feel comfortable and safe. It must have been something about the space, the energy, the people. I smiled slightly as it struck me: Everyone here was Asian American.

It turned out that Sokla was there sort of by accident too. He didn't know he was signing up to participate in a video-making project; he just heard there was a party in Chinatown. Nearly 4 years after I first met him in that teal blue room, Sokla told me about how it was also somewhat of an accident that he ended up in the United States. In the opening quote, Sokla explained that unlike other Asian Americans, who voluntarily immigrated, refugees from Southeast Asia (Cambodia, Laos, and Vietnam) did not intentionally set out to move to the United States; a war largely outside of their control was to blame. His family fled from Cambodia to a refugee camp on the Cambodian-Thai border where Sokla was later born. After securing a family sponsor on his mother's side, they moved to the United States when he was 5 years old. Sokla often created new identity labels to set his coming-to-America experience as a Southeast Asian refugee apart from that of other Asian immigrants, particularly Chinese and Japanese Americans. When guest speakers at the video-making project insisted that the youth participants were Asian American, for example, many of them refused this label and instead asserted that they were simply "Asian," either because they were not born in the United States or because they primarily ate Asian foods, spoke Asian languages, and associated with Asian people. As the argument continued, Sokla finally said, "Just say I'm the new wave of Asian Americans." A few years later, Sokla coined yet another new label, the "Other

Asian," to capture this same idea. By drawing on the Other Asian refugee experience with warfare and destitution as "other" than the Asian American immigrant belief in opportunity and meritocracy, Sokla explained to me the very problems with a panethnic Asian American identity. I smiled slightly as it struck me: Not everyone here was Asian American.

ASIAN AMERICAN IDENTITY: HISTORICAL, POLITICAL, AND INTERACTIONAL PERSPECTIVES

Complicating the panethnic capacity of the term "Asian American," Sokla pointed out something scholars in Asian American studies have long noted: As a panethnic unifying marker in theory, Asian American can also be understood as one of divisiveness in practice. Initially, the label "Asian American" was imposed by U.S. governmental agencies and news media to lump diverse Asian ethnic groups (e.g., Filipino, Korean, Vietnamese, Indian) into one monolithic category, thus eliding the profound cultural and linguistic differences between them (Espiritu, 1992). Other umbrella terms, such as "Hispanic" or "Latino," "Black" or "African American," and "American Indian" or "Native American," were also created and used to assemble diverse peoples into one of four groups to assist in the regulation and allocation of governmental services (Lowry, 1982). During the civil rights movement in the 1960s, however, minority activists began embracing these panethnic labels in the belief that building large coalitions inclusive of several ethnic groups would help advance political struggles for power and resources (Espiritu, 1992). Based on shared experiences with racism and disenfranchisement, Asian American activists appropriated the Asian American label to create a unified identity that allowed diverse Asian ethnic groups to join together and produce more numbers behind a united voice. The social life of the term "Asian American," then, exemplifies how panethnic identity is a product of various historical and political processes and not the result of shared cultural ties (Lopez & Espiritu, 1990).

Although the Asian American label was once imposed and then embraced, the initial debate about how a panethnic identity is even possible with such inner group heterogeneity has never been resolved. Lowe (1996) explains how the formation of an Asian American identity in response to racial politics is still problematic:

[W]hile Asian American cultural identity emerges in the context of the racialized exclusion of Asian immigrants from enfranchisement in the political and
cultural spheres of the United States, important contradictions exist between an
exclusively Asian American cultural nationalist construction of identity and the
material heterogeneity of the Asian American constituency, particularly class,
gender, and national-origin differences among peoples of Asian descent in the
United States. (p. 38)

Lowe (1996) argues that the diversity between and within Asian ethnic groups
complicates a unified formation of Asian American identity. This fragmentation
is largely due to both external and internal power struggles: external because the
U.S. government and media assign racial labels to Asian ethnic groups; internal
because various Asian ethnic groups fight for inclusion in or exclusion from the
panethnic label. Although some agree that Asian Americans are people of East
Asian (Korean, Chinese, etc.), Southeast Asian (Lao, Cambodian, etc.), and
South Asian (Indian, Sri Lankan, etc.) descent in the United States, the term
"Asian American" is still commonly understood by many people, including
Sokla, as only representing the interests of Chinese and Japanese Americans
(Espiritu, 1992, pp. 50–51). For Sokla, his conviction was rooted in what he per-
ceived as a fundamental distinction between Asian Americans and the Other
Asian, a distinction based on immigration history and socioeconomic status. Be-
cause his experiences and politics were not represented or shared by an Asian
American agenda, he often chose to exclude himself from the label.

Similar issues surround other groups. Should South Asian Americans form
a separate group apart from Asian Americans? Are Filipino Americans Asian
American, Pacific Islander American, or something else? Should Pacific Island-
ers (Samoan, Micronesian, etc.) who immigrated to the United States be lumped
together with Asian Americans? Should the term "Asian American" be replaced
by Asian Pacific American, Asian Pacific Islander American, or Asian and Pacific Islander American? Although asking such questions often elicits passionate
responses, there are no definitive answers. The central issue here is that the
panethnic Asian American identity is a shifting, social negotiation rather than an
enduring, fixed entity. Bureaucrats, scholars, activists, and everyday people like
Sokla contribute to this contentious debate, which will likely continue for many
years to come.

In addition to larger historical and political processes that shape the formation of identity, everyday social interaction is an equally powerful force through

which people position themselves as certain types of people. Much linguistic anthropological research reveals that far from being fixed attributes of individuals, identities are achieved through the constant interplay between larger macrolevel processes—which influence the social categories available to individuals—and local interactional processes—which allow individuals to construct their identities within these larger constraints (e.g., Bailey, 2002; Bucholtz & Hall, 2003; Rampton, 1995a). Repertoires of identities are taken as the norm, and people play with a variety of linguistic devices through which identities are accomplished in interaction (e.g., M. Goodwin, 1999; Kroskrity, 1993).

For example, Southeast Asian refugees, like Sokla, have access to a multitude of labels that provide a range of ways to construct their identities. At one time or another, Sokla has identified as "Asian," "Other Asian," "Cambodian," "American," even "Asian American." Such labels are not simply denotational names for groups; they achieve complex levels of meaning within specific contexts of use (Rymes, 1996). For example, Sokla may identify as "Cambodian" to claim an ethnic identity when talking to other Asian Americans, as "Asian American" to assert a political identity when talking to European Americans, or as the "Other Asian" to emphasize distinctions between Asian American groups when talking to a researcher. The use of labels can even accomplish multiple effects: Identifying as "Asian" can simultaneously deny allegiance to an American identity and distance oneself from self-identified Asian Americans.

Yet to reveal what meanings and identities actually emerge in interaction, close analysis of situated discourse is crucial. With this perspective on language use, I argue that it was not that Sokla opposed the Asian American label itself; rather, his opposition was shaped by aspects of the interactional context: who he was talking to, where the conversation took place, what topics were being discussed, and so on. Taking a linguistic approach to identity in this study, I examined conversations at the after-school video-making project and discovered that Sokla and several other teenagers often used stereotypes as resources for constructing their identities and relationships with others. This book explores this intersection of language, identity, and stereotype.

ASIAN AMERICAN STEREOTYPES: SOCIETAL CIRCULATION
AND LOCAL EMERGENCE

Similar to the formation of Asian American identity, Asian American stereotypes are also produced through historical, political, and interactional processes. Social scientific research on stereotypes dates back to Lippmann (1922), who referred to them as pictures in the heads of individuals looking out into their social world. He argued that people interact directly not with objective reality but with the representations they have created about that reality. Since Lippmann, most stereotype research has been carried out by social psychologists (e.g., Leyens, Yzerbyt, & Schadron, 1994; Maass & Arcuri, 1992; Stangor & Schaller, 1996), who generally agree on two core characteristics of stereotypes: their necessity and their sharedness. First, without stereotypes, people would move about the world in a rather inefficient manner, unable to draw on prior understandings of objects or people. Fetching a glass of water, for example, would be a slow task if people could not access the stereotype of water as transparent, drinkable liquid. Second, for typifications—links made between attributes (e.g., transparent) and entities (e.g., water)—to develop into stereotypes, they must be shared at the level of groups or societies. Although it is not entirely clear to what degree a typification must be shared for it to qualify as a stereotype, social psychologists agree that the mass media is a powerful mechanism through which stereotypes are disseminated across national and global scales (e.g., Katz & Bradley, 1933; Wilson & Gutierrez, 1985).

Linguistic anthropologists offer a promising approach to understanding how stereotypes are formed and disseminated through the concept of circulation (Agha, 2003; Bauman & Briggs, 1990; Silverstein & Urban, 1996). Language use is central to how a typification develops into a stereotype through its circulation in a speech chain network consisting of senders and receivers (Agha, 2003). In a speech chain, a sender transmits a message to a receiver, who in turn becomes a sender who transmits it to another receiver and so on. The existence of a stereotype, then, relies on continuous streams of speech chains; otherwise, a stereotype can fade if speech chains break, they become filled with countermessages, or their senders and receivers die out.[2] A single transaction between a sender and receiver can be as small as a dyadic interaction between, for example, a speaker and a hearer in face-to-face conversation. A single transaction can also disseminate instantly across societies between, for example, a news broadcast and millions of viewers. Such wide-scale transmission in various mass media—such as film, music, newspapers, and advertisements—is rarely neutral because those who control the messages and the media through which messages circulate play a powerful role in the political economy of texts (Gal, 1989; Irvine, 1989). Accounting for both the stability and fragility of stereotypes, this model of circulation acknowledges the significance of different levels of dissemination, from wide-scale speech chains controlled by a privileged few to small-scale speech chains among a local community, such as the participants at the after-school video-making project, which is the focus of this study.

Scholars in Asian American studies have also contributed to the research literature on stereotypes. Given the political activism that gave rise to the field, Asian Americanists focus on stereotypes of persons—namely Asian Americans—and view such stereotypes as largely negative and false ideas used by the dominant majority to oppress minority groups. Research in this area examines how Asian American stereotypes reflect the unique ways in which Asian Americans are positioned in U.S. racial discourses. Because the national obsession with race is usually framed in Black-White terms, scholars argue that Asian Americans are left to be perceived as either forever foreigners or honorary Whites (Tuan, 1998)—as not belonging in the United States or as similar to the dominant majority.

Forever Foreigner Stereotype

The stereotype of the forever foreigner draws on discourses of Orientalism, ideologies which shape the image of Asian and Middle Eastern peoples as Other and thus unassimable due to innate East-West differences that cannot be re-

---

[2]This does not mean, however, that stereotypes cannot be revived. For instance, Gilbert (1951) found that in 1933, Princeton students thought that the Japanese were intelligent, industrious, and progressive, but in 1951, they saw the Japanese as sly and shrewd. Then, in 1969, other researchers showed that the stereotypes had returned to what they were in 1933 (Leyens et al., 1994). This example reveals the cyclical nature of some stereotypes as dictated by historical events, such as the Japanese defeat of the Russians in 1904, World War II, and Japan's emerging presence in the global economy in the 1960s.

solved (Said, 1978). Despite that people of Asian descent have been in the United States since at least the California gold rush in 1848 (Takaki, 1989)—and as early as 1571, when the Spanish brought Chinese shipbuilders to California and Filipino seamen to Louisiana (Fong, 1998)—Asian Americans continue to be perceived as the foreigner-within (Lowe, 1996). That Asian Americans are not accepted as American is illustrated by just one of many examples from my fieldwork: One day, a European American woman asked Narun, a Thai Cambodian Chinese American girl, where she was from, speaking in a slowly articulated manner as if assuming that Narun's first language was not English. After Narun replied "South Philly," the woman appeared irritated and asked again, "No, where are you *really* from?" Unfortunately, this unwillingness to accept that someone who looks Asian can also be American is not unfamiliar to many Asian Americans, even though some have families that have been in the United States for five or more generations.

Playing no small role in nurturing the forever foreigner stereotype is the mass media, which often depicts Asian Americans as an alien presence that threatens, disrupts, and pollutes the internal structure of cultural formation in the United States (R. Lee, 1999). Two early films portraying Asian immigrants—Cecil B. De Mille's *The Cheat* (1915) and D. W. Griffith's *Broken Blossoms* (1919)—although popular in their time, have recently been criticized for perpetuating the permanent alien image (Marchetti, 1993; Moy, 1992). These and other later films, such as *Sayonara* (1957) by Joshua Logan, portray Asians as the "yellow peril" through the sexual threat of miscegenation, tainting White racial "purity" with foreign blood (Hagedorn, 1994; Marchetti, 1993). Though largely absent from contemporary entertainment media, Asian Americans do occasionally appear; however, they are rarely depicted as second generation Americans but instead as conniving or socially awkward foreigners with accented English or a proclivity for martial arts (Fong, 1998; Hamamoto, 1994; R. Lee, 1999). This imbalanced and misleading representation of Asian Americans—nearly half of whom are American born (Reeves & Bennett, 2004)—helps maintain the image of the forever foreigner in U.S. racial discourses.

News media coverage of the thriving Japanese auto industry in the 1980s and of the campaign finance scandals involving foreign Asian donors in the 1990s are just two more recent examples continuing a long tradition of perceived Asian threats. Such fear often results in discriminatory U.S. policies,

policies that date back to the Chinese Exclusion Law in 1882, when Chinese immigrant laborers were seen as threatening the employability of White Americans (Takaki, 1989). This Asian-as-foreign-threat perception is applied not only to Asians in Asia but also to Asian Americans, as illustrated by the brutal killing of Vincent Chin in 1982 by White unemployed Detroit autoworkers who thought he was Japanese. That Chin was Chinese American was of little concern to these men who assumed he was foreign and thus a threat to their livelihood.

Fig. 1.1 illustrates a pair of oppositions that situates the forever foreigner stereotype of Asian Americans in U.S. racial discourses. Whereas the first opposition is based on a Black-White binary, the second opposition is based on an American-foreign binary. Although African Americans and European Americans are set in opposition to each other, they are both seen as American. Asian Americans, on the other hand, are set in opposition to both groups because they are commonly perceived as foreign, not American.

Honorary White Stereotype

Standing in seeming contradiction, the honorary White stereotype coexists with the forever foreigner stereotype. The honorary White image portrays Asian Americans as succeeding in U.S. society along with the White dominant majority, undergoing both a literal and metaphorical process of "whitening" as White-Asian intermarriage rates increase and the Confucian work ethic that

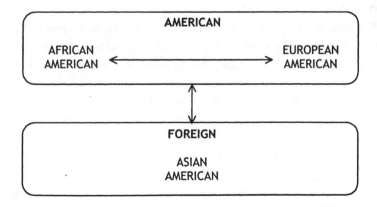

FIG. 1.1 Asian Americans as forever foreigners in U.S. racial discourses.

Asian immigrants supposedly bring with them meshes neatly with American ideologies of hard work and meritocracy (Tuan, 1998).

The honorary White stereotype is based on the model minority myth, which explicitly emerged in the 1960s but had its origins in the Cold War (R. Lee, 1999). In the 1940s and 1950s, Asian Americans were sometimes depicted as a successful case of ethnic assimilation to help contain "the red menace of communism, the black menace of racial integration, and the white menace of homosexuality" (R. Lee, 1999, p. 10). It was no accident, then, that the model minority stereotype later emerged explicitly during the civil rights movement with the help of news media, such as *U.S. News and World Report*'s portrayal of Asian Americans as a "success story" in a December 1966 article. During the 1960s the honorary White image was used to silence accusations of racial injustice as African, Latino, and Native American communities were left to blame only themselves for not achieving the same supposed success as Asian Americans, their fellow minorities.

At first glance, the model minority myth is seemingly flattering because it creates a smart and successful—but quiet and obedient—image for Asian Americans. Yet numerous Asian Americans struggle economically and academically, and this stereotype of success becomes dangerous because it silences the experiences of the many Asian Americans who do not fit this image. The model minority myth is thus a powerful mechanism for upholding U.S. ideologies of meritocracy and individualism, diverting attention away from racial inequality, sustaining Whites in the racial hierarchy, and pitting minority groups against each other (S. Lee, 1996).

Not only is the honorary White stereotype sustained by political currents, but it is also ignited by some academic discourses on U.S. minorities. In what has been called the cultural ecological framework, Ogbu (1974, 1978) distinguishes between so-called voluntary and involuntary minorities. According to Ogbu, voluntary minorities (e.g., Asian Americans) come to the United States willingly in search of a better life, whereas involuntary minorities (e.g., Hawaiians, African Americans) are forced into minority status through conquest and enslavement. Because of the different histories, identities, perceptions of future opportunities, and views of education between these two groups, voluntary minorities tend to do well in school because they see it as a necessary step to success (Gibson, 1988; Suárez-Orozco, 1991), whereas involuntary minorities often reject school because of their distrust in Whites and disbelief in the possibility of social mobility (Ogbu, 1978).

Yet much research has challenged the homogenizing nature of the cultural ecological model, given that Asian Americans are not one monolithic mass of voluntary minorities who succeed in schools (e.g., Hune & Chan, 1999; Kiang, 1996; S. Lee, 1996; Nakanishi & Hirano-Nakanishi, 1983; Takaki, 1989; Trueba, Cheng, & Ima, 1993). As Sokla pointed out, the Other Asians hardly come to the United States voluntarily, yet they are often lumped together with Asian Americans who did. Although Ogbu was initially writing before the mass influx of post-1975 Southeast Asian refugees, Asian Americans were already a heterogeneous group. As he draws on his own research of successful Chinese, Filipino, and Japanese Americans in the 1960s (Ogbu, 1974, 1977), he invokes the panethnic Asian American label to generalize about all Asian American ethnic groups, though they varied profoundly—both between and within groups—in terms of socioeconomic status and educational achievement. Such academic discourses coupled with popular perceptions have largely ignored the diverse and complex experiences of Asian Americans who do not fit the image of honorary White success.

Fig. 1.2 expands on Fig. 1.1 to illustrate how the honorary White stereotype aligns Asian Americans more closely to European Americans, as represented by

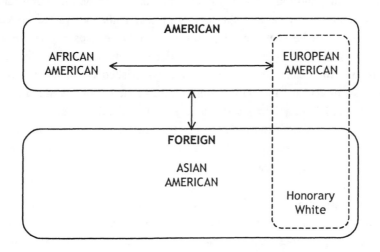

FIG. 1.2 Asian Americans as forever foreigners and honorary Whites
in U.S. racial discourses.

the dotted circle that groups them together and sets them in opposition to African Americans. Rather than seeing the forever foreigner and honorary White stereotypes as mutually exclusive, however, I see the perception of foreigner as a larger organizing principle within which the model minority myth operates. For example, honorary Whites are still seen as foreign through the explanation of Asian American success as an immigrant—thus foreign—ideology of hard work brought with them to the United States. Because I am not claiming that Asian Americans as model minorities are always perceived as foreign, the dotted circle, which reaches across the American-foreign binary, allows for occasional leakage of an American identity onto Asian Americans.

Problem Minority Stereotype

What is missing from this forever foreigner–honorary White picture, however, is a deep investigation of a third emerging stereotype: that which positions Asian Americans not as model minority but as problem minority (cf. Peters, 1988, on Southeast Asian refugee "problem youth"). Because the Black-White paradigm dominates U.S. racial discourses, African Americans have been the ones principally burdened with the image of the problem minority. Societal discourses often depict African Americans as criminals, drug dealers, social welfare parasites, deadbeat dads, and thus "problems" that supposedly erode the moral fabric of American society by perpetuating cycles of social ills and wasted tax dollars. Yet recently Southeast Asian refugees (among other groups, e.g., some Latino Americans) have fallen prey to these familiar stereotypes traditionally assigned to African Americans, as they settle in impoverished urban areas across the United States and participate in gang culture in New York (Chin, 1996), Los Angeles (Vigil & Yun, 1990), and other major cities (Badey, 1988).

Data gleaned from the U.S. Census Bureau further support this emerging stereotype of Cambodian, Lao, Hmong (from highland Laos), Vietnamese, and ethnic Chinese from Southeast Asia as poor, uneducated, and deviant. Tables 1.1 and 1.2, which present statistics from the 2000 U.S. Census, reveal how Southeast Asian Americans fare compared with European Americans, African Americans, and other Asian Americans in terms of education and poverty. Looking at educational achievement across racial groups in Table 1.1, the Asian American model minority stereotype seems to hold true: Asian Americans attain more

TABLE 1.1

Educational Attainment by Racial and Ethnic Group of People Ages 25 and Over
in the United States in 2000

	Percent High School Graduate or Higher	Percent Bachelor's Degree or Higher
Total U.S. population	80.4	24.4
Racial groups		
European American	83.4	25.9
African American	71.3	14.2
Asian American	80.6	42.7
Asian ethnic groups		
Indian American	85.4	60.9
Chinese American	77.6	46.6
Filipino American	87.4	41.7
Japanese American	91.4	40.4
Korean American	86.4	43.1
Cambodian American	47.1	9.1
Hmong American	40.7	7.4
Laotian American	50.5	7.6
Vietnamese American	61.9	19.5

Note. From Southeast Asian American Statistical Profile (p. 15), by M. Niedzwiecki
and T. C. Duong, 2004, Washington, DC: Southeast Asia Resource Action Center. Copyright 2003 by Southeast Asia Resource Action Center.

education than both European Americans and African Americans. Likewise, in
Table 1.2, although both European Americans and Asian Americans have similarly low poverty rates, twice as many African Americans live in poverty as
Asian Americans. Those looking only at racial groups would walk away thinking that Asian Americans are doing exceptionally well: On the surface they do
indeed appear to be model minorities, sometimes even "outwhiting" Whites.

However, this picture drastically changes when Asian Americans are broken into ethnic groups. For example, all Southeast Asian Americans fall far be-
low the percentage of Asian American college graduates, leaving Cambodian,
Hmong, and Laotian Americans much less likely to graduate from college than

TABLE 1.2

Poverty Status by Racial and Ethnic Group in the United States in 1999

	Percent Living Below Federal Poverty Line
Total U.S. population	12.4
Racial groups	
European American	9.4
African American	24.7
Asian American	12.6
Asian ethnic groups	
Indian American	10.4
Chinese American	13.2
Filipino American	7.0
Japanese American	9.2
Korean American	14.2
Cambodian American	29.3
Hmong American	37.6
Laotian American	19.1
Vietnamese American	16.0

Note. From Southeast Asian American Statistical Profile (p. 15), by M. Niedzwiecki and T. C. Duong, 2004, Washington, DC: Southeast Asia Resource Action Center. Copyright 2003 by Southeast Asia Resource Action Center.

even African Americans. In fact, African Americans are more likely to graduate from high school than all Southeast Asian American groups. A similar picture emerges when looking at poverty levels. All Southeast Asian Americans have much higher poverty rates than the average Asian American. Moreover, Cambodian and Hmong Americans have higher rates of poverty than African Americans. These statistics—and not the model minority myth—draw a more accurate picture of how Southeast Asian Americans participate in the U.S. economy and educational system. These numbers, however, do not draw a complete picture, given their inability to explore the diverse experiences and perspectives of Cambodian, Hmong, Laotian, and Vietnamese Americans.

Fig. 1.3 further expands on Figs. 1.1 and 1.2 by illustrating how the emergence of the problem minority stereotype aligns the Other Asian more closely to the location of African Americans in U.S. racial discourses. Completing this picture is the emergence of a third opposition between problem minorities and honorary Whites, which parallels the Black-White opposition. Just like honorary Whites, problem minorities are often seen as foreign given the common perception of Southeast Asian Americans as foreign-born refugees.

Although Mia Tuan (1998) and Stacey Lee (1996) both cite studies, data, or statistics that discredit the stereotypes of Asian Americans as forever foreigners and honorary Whites, neither author focuses on how Asian Americans are situated relative to the problem minority stereotype. Tuan looked exclusively at middle-class Chinese and Japanese Americans, and Lee investigated several different Asian ethnic groups but only in an academically oriented high school, where the model minority myth weighed most heavily on their lives. More recent work explores how the experiences of Southeast Asian American youth are shaped by the problem minority stereotype, for example, Hmong Americans as delinquents (S. Lee, 2001) and Laotian Americans as gangsters (Bucholtz, 2004). This book builds on this recent work by examining primarily low-income Southeast Asian American youth who were being failed by or pushed out (Fine, 1991) of low-performing public high schools and whose experiences and perspectives were affected by the problem minority stereotype. Moving beyond the limitations of U.S. Census statistics, this book combines ethnography with the

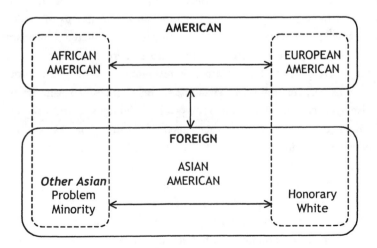

FIG. 1.3 Asian Americans as forever foreigners, honorary Whites, and problem minorities in U.S. racial discourses.

close analysis of interaction to explore the local ways in which these teens constructed their identities in a unique alternative educational setting designed specifically for them. Because the meaning of Asian American identity was complicated by the emergence of the Other Asian, this book partly examines how the intersection of racial and socioeconomic factors shaped the ways in which these Southeast Asian American youth positioned themselves relative to African American urban youth culture and to the problem minority stereotype.

Local Emergence of Stereotypes

Although the forever foreigner, honorary White, and problem minority stereotypes circulate to varying degrees at the societal level, the ways in which they are invoked as local models in the performance and interpretation of identities can be examined at the interactional level. Following Putnam (1975), who describes a stereotype as a typical feature of a kind, I broadly define stereotypes as widespread typifications linking attributes to entities. Yet this book is less interested in how stereotypes circulate among large-scale social groups and more interested in how individuals make sense and use of stereotypes at the level of interaction.

Specifically, I am interested in what stereotypes mean to the Southeast Asian American teenagers in this study. I found that there was no agreed-on meaning of what a stereotype was and that the various meanings often depended on the interactional contexts in which stereotypes were invoked. For example, at times stereotypes were perceived as inaccurate representations, and at other times they were perceived as negative representations. When stereotypes were understood as perpetuating only inaccurate things about Asian Americans, some teens displayed confusion when stereotypes had elements of truth or relevance to their lives (e.g., when the teens found themselves fitting the Asian storeowner stereotype because their families owned stores). Likewise, when stereotypes were understood as perpetuating only negative things about Asian Americans, some teens displayed confusion when stereotypes seemed to reflect positively on Asian people (e.g., when the teens perceived the Asian martial arts stereotype as favorably depicting Asian Americans as strong and formidable). At times stereotypes were seen as oppressive, but at other times they were appropriated as sources of power, humor, and in-group cohesiveness. These various understandings of stereotypes made me aware of how slippery and elusive the concept of stereotype was. I became interested in how different interactional conditions brought about different interpretations of stereotypes and how stereotypes could be useful in the construction of youth identities.

This book examines how the Southeast Asian American teenagers often interactionally invoked both stereotypes of the self and other as they explored and produced their identities. Because most research focuses on how stereotypes are applied by one group onto another, the misperception of stereotyping as something that is only done to others is fueled. In this line of thinking, people struggle to define themselves outside of the forceful grip that stereotypes hold on popular perception. Although research pays less attention to how people stereotype themselves, this process is actually implicit given that people are partly defined by how they define others, that is, by what they are not (cf. Hall, 1996). There has been some social psychological work on self-stereotyping (e.g., Tajfel, 1978; Turner, 1982), which examines how people apply stereotypes to themselves through concepts such as social differentiation (Tajfel, 1981), where people assign more favorable judgments onto the groups that they identify with, and speech accommodation theory (later renamed communication accommodation theory) (Giles, Taylor, & Bourhis, 1973), where people alter their speech according to stereotypic beliefs about how in-group and out-group members talk.

Some anthropological research on schooling has also examined how groups can apply stereotypes to themselves. Stacey Lee (1996), for example, explored how Asian American high school students apply the model minority stereotype to their own lives, albeit in service to a hegemonic order that ultimately oppresses them. Foley (1996) examined a similar phenomenon—how Mesquaki high school students apply the "silent Indian" stereotype to themselves—and found that this practice can be a situational strategy for achieving local goals, such as manipulating White liberal teachers to leave them alone. What I hope to do in this book is further explore this interplay between socially circulating stereotypes and how individuals make use of them in their own lives. Although stereotypes are commonly perceived as oppressive, I argue that they can also be empowering, as illustrated by the ways in which the Southeast Asian American teens in this study creatively applied stereotypes to themselves and to others in the construction of their own identities.

OVERVIEW OF THE RESEARCH PROCESS

If it was an accident that Sokla came to the United States and also to the video-making project, it hardly seemed like an accident when 5 years later this Other Asian graduated from college with a major in film and media arts. I attended Sokla's high school graduation ceremony where he had already beaten the statistic that less than half of Cambodian Americans attain a high school degree. And despite the staggering odds against him that less than a tenth of Cambodian Americans graduate from college, Sokla did it. The video-making project Sokla accidentally attended introduced him to something he passionately pursued for many years. Majoring in film and media arts at a large university, he moved on from the video-making project to independently produce, write, direct, and edit more videos. This was the ultimate dream of the organizers of the video-making project, who had hoped to influence the lives of young Southeast Asian Americans.

This book draws on data collected over the entire 4-year life span of the after-school video-making project (1999–2002). With the belief that researchers are part of the social world they study, I chose to conduct ethnographic research, drawing heavily on linguistic anthropology to examine the perspectives of Asian American youth as they discursively constructed their identities in relation to stereotypes. In addition to being a participant-observer, writing field notes, collecting site documents, and conducting interviews, I audio- and video-recorded interactions among the teenagers during project sessions of the video-making project and in various other settings, such as conferences and film festivals, where the teens interacted with others about the video-making project.

Entering the Research Site and Negotiating My Role

In the fall of 1998, I met Bi (Vietnamese American female), then a graduate student in public health, at a local Vietnamese American organization in Philadelphia. At the organization, I was a work-study student through my graduate school. My various duties included writing grants, teaching an English as a second language (ESL) class for Vietnamese American adults, and supervising an after-school program for Vietnamese American children at a nearby public elementary school. As Bi and I became friends, I told her about how I used to be a supervisor of an after-school program for Hmong refugee youth in Lansing,

Michigan, and that I was hoping to carry out my dissertation research with a similar population in a similar educational setting. Bi told me about a group of medical students she was involved with who were preparing to launch an after-school video-making project for Southeast Asian refugee youth in February, 1999. She put me in contact with one of the main organizers, Ike (Chinese American male), who interviewed me over the telephone before inviting me to volunteer for the video-making project. I arrived on the first day of the video-making project and continued to return for 4 years.

Over the 4 years of my fieldwork, I took on various roles at the video-making project and at the Asian Arts Initiative,[3] the Asian American community arts organization where the video-making project took place. For the first 2 years (1999, 2000), I was an unpaid volunteer at the video-making project, coming to the field site once or twice a week and helping to organize, implement, and evaluate weekly project sessions. During the first two summers, I was a paid intern, working full-time as the postproduction and curriculum development coordinator for the video-making project. In the 3rd year (2001), I was a paid staff member at the Asian Arts Initiative, working an average of 10 hr a week as a Youth Arts Workshop Coordinator, writing grants and directing the video-making project and other after-school programs for the organization. In the final year of the video-making project (2002), I decided to gain a different perspective by taking a step back and simply being a researcher with no decision-making role. I went to the field site an average of twice a week during this final project year.

In addition to my many institutional identities at the video-making project, I also had to balance my role as researcher. This was difficult at times because I often found myself being equally interested in conducting my research and working for an organization I cared deeply about. As a result, some staff members and teenagers viewed me as a "softy" because, as a researcher, my desire to listen to stories and develop relationships with the teens sometimes compromised my ability to do my job. For example, when I was a Youth Arts Workshop coordinator, a paid staff position, one of my responsibilities was to supervise the work-study students. Sokla, who at the time was a freshman in college, was one of the work-study students under my supervision. If he didn't arrive to work on time or didn't carry out his responsibilities, I found myself hesitating to

---

[3]The Asian Arts Initiative has requested that the name of the organization not be changed in publications resulting from this research.

discipline him in fear that it would jeopardize our close relationship and affect his willingness to be a research participant. Such struggles were difficult to manage as an ethnographer who was constantly trying to balance her role as both participant and researcher.

During most of my fieldwork, I felt as though the teenagers and staff members viewed me as any other volunteer or program coordinator at the Asian Arts Initiative. This might have been the case because I was often engrossed in my volunteer and work responsibilities at the organization and because my youthful appearance, ethnic background (Filipino European American female), and interest in Asian American issues fit the part of any other volunteer or staff member. Also, no one had ever conducted extensive research at the organization so "researcher" was not a familiar role to participants. Of course at times—particularly at the beginning of each project year when I explained my research, sent the participants home with consent forms, set up video cameras and audio tape recorders, and walked around with a notebook into which I scribbled furiously—my role as researcher became more visible. But I found that after a few weeks, the teenagers became quite used to my recording devices and ended up largely ignoring them. I believe this was partly because there was a lot of other video equipment around that was being used in the video-making project.

I developed close relationships with several teens and staff members over the course of my fieldwork. During project sessions, the teens often opened up about their hopes and struggles with regard to their lives, futures, and relationships with families, friends, and peers. The video-making project produced an overall atmosphere of community and closeness where relationships among teens and adults were easily fostered. The teens certainly saw me and the other project volunteers and staff members as adults—or "old heads" as they liked to call us—but we were adults whom they tended to confide in and socialize with before, during, and after project sessions. If I arrived early to a project session, sometimes a teen and I would grab Chinese pastry and bubble tea in Chinatown. After project sessions, I would sometimes join a small group of teens and adults for dinner. I would also socialize with teens on days when there was no project session: for example, at a Filipino American boy band concert, at the premiere of the latest *Star Wars* film, at the New Jersey shore during the Asian Arts Initiative staff retreat, and at a birthday party for one of the teen participants. I also hosted the annual video-making project end-of-year party at my apartment each summer. In addition to socializing, I wrote recommendation letters for teens who were applying to colleges and for scholarships and gave teens feedback on their artwork and writing. I also developed some close friendships with staff members and project volunteers that continue today.

Formation of the Video-making Project

With an enthusiastic commitment to Asian American issues and community organizing, a small group of Asian American medical and public health students in Philadelphia decided to develop a program in 1999 that would engage local Southeast Asian refugee youth. The five students—Ike (Chinese American male), Bi and Nina (Vietnamese American females), and Rosette and Mona (Filipino American females)—were driven by their concern over reports of high dropout, drug abuse, gang participation, and suicide rates among Southeast Asian American teenagers. Their goal was to design a project that would involve young people in identifying, exploring, and addressing issues that the youth saw as important to their own communities and to foster problem-solving capacities and a sense of pride, accomplishment, and self-esteem among young Southeast Asian Americans. After deliberating over the kinds of projects they could develop, the medical students decided to create an after-school video-making project, which, according to a grant proposal they wrote, sought to empower Southeast Asian youth by meeting the following criteria:

- Provides a culturally specific alternative to traditional after-school programs
- Generates awareness of health and social issues relevant to Southeast Asian youth
- Facilitates participants' recognition of the interrelationships between education and good health
- Helps participants develop practical skills in media, health, and education that are applicable to future educational and career endeavors
- Stimulates dialogue and reflection in the youth and in the greater community during screenings of finished video productions
- Provides internship and leadership opportunities for participants

Partnering with the Asian Arts Initiative, a local Asian American community arts organization, which provided administrative support and the physical space for the video-making project, the medical students wrote and received a grant from a local grassroots video organization, which provided the video equipment and supplies and two video instructors. The medical students also arranged with the public schools for participation in the video-making project to fulfill the mandatory community service requirement for high school students.

After securing funding and resources, the project organizers created a curriculum. The video-making project was designed to accommodate around 15 teenagers, 6 adult volunteers, and 2 video instructors or teaching artists who would meet every Tuesday from 3:30–6:00 p.m. from February to May 1999. The program was divided into two major phases. In the first phase, project sessions consisted of two parts. In the first part, a different guest speaker would share his or her experiences about one of the following themes: drug and alcohol abuse, HIV/AIDS and sexually transmitted diseases, date rape, anti-Asian violence and gang violence, and Asian American identity. The medical students planned for these sessions to be interactive and not didactic, allowing youth to contribute their ideas, thoughts, opinions, and reactions. In the second part of each meeting, the two video instructors would teach video skills and techniques, including principles of camera operation, sound, and lighting. The teens would also view and critique short videos to begin thinking about the type of video story they would like to create. In the second phase of the video-making project, the teens would start working together to select one health or social theme for their 15-min fictional or documentary story. In April and May, the teens would write the script, then film the video. The two video instructors, with the assistance of one or two teen participants, would be principally involved in editing the video in time for the November public screening that would be arranged by the local grassroots video organization. The medical students had hopes that the video would be screened at additional venues, including classrooms, conferences, community organizations, and film festivals. They also had hopes that the video-making project would be offered in future years to new groups of Southeast Asian American youth. Both of these hopes were realized.

After the curriculum was designed, the medical students set out to recruit teen participants. They concentrated their recruitment efforts at public high schools in poor urban neighborhoods in South Philadelphia, areas with high concentrations of Southeast Asian refugees. The medical students worked with Dr. Don (Japanese American male), a high school advisor for Asian American students, who arranged for them to present this opportunity to Southeast Asian

American teenagers during school hours. On February 9, 1999, the project began, and 18 teenagers showed up.

Teen Participants

All 18 teen participants that arrived on the first day of the video-making project
were from families that had immigrated from Cambodia, Vietnam, or Laos. The
teens and their families were like many other post-1975 Southeast Asian refugees who escaped the hardships of war, poverty, and brutal conditions in their
home countries and first-asylum camps only to face poverty, unemployment,
and racism in the United States.

The connection between the U.S. government and Southeast Asian refugee
resettlement dates back to the 1950s. In 1954, the United States played a large
part in encouraging, funding, and carrying out the resettlement of nearly one
million Vietnamese from communist-controlled North Vietnam to pro-U.S. gov-
ernment-run South Vietnam (Tollefson, 1989). With this began the central role
taken by the United States to control the spread of communism in Southeast
Asia. Additional efforts included the increased U.S. military presence and inces-
sant bombing of Laos and rural areas of South Vietnam in the mid-1960s and the
heavy recruitment of Hmong soldiers to serve and die for U.S. political interests
(Tollefson, 1989). But in 1975, South Vietnam eventually succumbed to the
military prowess of communist-run North Vietnam, causing the United States to
pull out while communism continued to take over. Later that year, the commu-
nist Pathet Lao defeated the U.S.-supported Lao government, and in 1976 the
U.S.-backed Cambodian government collapsed under the notorious Khmer
Rouge. From 1975 to 2002, nearly 1.5 million refugees from Vietnam, Cambodia, and Laos resettled in the United States, primarily in urban areas, such as
Philadelphia (Niedzwiecki & Duong, 2004).

In the first few weeks of the video-making project, discussions and activi-
ties created opportunities for these Southeast Asian American youth to reveal
themselves as the type of teen the project organizers hoped to reach. Some were
in gangs. Some were victims or perpetrators of violent crimes. Some carried
weapons. Some had just been released from prison. Some used drugs and drank
alcohol. Some were getting bad grades. Some had dropped out of school. The
participants in this book were like the "real new wavers" (friends of the Asian
American new wave students in Stacey Lee's 1996 study), "who drank, gam-

bled, carried weapons, and belonged to gangs" (p. 40). Although the majority of teen participants at the video-making project were second generation, meaning they were American born to foreign-born parents, the rest of the teens would be considered "1.5 generation" (Portes, 1996; Rumbaut & Ima, 1988) because they were born in Southeast Asian countries or in refugee camps or processing centers in Thailand or the Philippines and then immigrated to the United States before adolescence, in most cases before the age of 5 years. All of the teens lived in poor neighborhoods in South Philadelphia, where many of them adopted clothing, speech, and lifestyles often associated with African American urban youth culture. Most of the teenagers gravitated toward hip hop music and culture, and many of the young men were avid breakdancers who also dabbled in graffiti art, rapping, DJ-ing, and R&B singing and songwriting.

But any homogeneous image of these young people quickly broke down as they revealed the different paths their lives were taking. Whereas some teens were being failed by schools, one teen was graduating as salutatorian of his high school. Whereas some aspired to be car mechanics, others aspired to be politicians. Whereas some teens had difficulty reading and writing, some including Sna (Cambodian American male), who said he could be inspired to write an entire story from any single word, composed poetry, plays, and scripts. Their opinions were equally heterogeneous, like when they debated over the virtue of sweatshop owners: Some argued that they provided much-needed employment to newly arrived immigrants, whereas others argued that they exploited vulnerable, disenfranchised workers.

To the chagrin of some of the original organizers, over its 4-year life span the video-making project increasingly attracted youth from "better" schools and neighborhoods. The project was originally conceived to serve teenagers who were struggling with school, gangs, drugs, and poverty. In the 1st and 2nd years, it met this goal. But in the 3rd and 4th years, this type of teenager was being outnumbered by youth who were doing better academically and socioeconomically. For example, although all teens in the 1st year lived in poor areas of South Philadelphia, over the years there were increasingly more teens from other parts of Philadelphia, including some middle-class neighborhoods. Moreover, although in the 1st project year all of the teen participants attended neighborhood schools, by the 4th project year, the majority of teens were from magnet schools. Neighborhood schools—particularly the ones attended by the teen participants—were regular public schools often with low academic standards and high violence and dropout rates, whereas magnet schools were prestigious, academically oriented public schools that required an entrance exam for admission. Most of the magnet school students in the video-making project maintained good grades and were college bound, whereas many neighborhood school students struggled academically and were planning to move directly into the workforce after high school.

This gradual shift from serving primarily neighborhood school students to magnet school students brought about an interesting meeting ground for teenagers who rarely crossed paths. One main difference between these two groups was the way in which the honorary White and problem minority stereotypes interacted with their lives: Whereas many magnet school students complained about teachers and peers comparing them to the model minority myth, the neighborhood school students expressed how others expected them to fit the image of the problem minority. This is illustrated by an example from my fieldwork when Anh (Vietnamese Cambodian Chinese American female), a magnet school student, and Moeun (Cambodian Chinese American male), a neighborhood school student, were asked by an adult volunteer what their teachers thought of them: Whereas Anh answered "smart," Moeun replied "dumb."

Throughout the 4-year life span of the video-making project, the majority of teen participants ethnically identified as Cambodian. A close second, however, were teens who identified as multiethnic. The teens often used the terms "pure," for those who identified with a single ethnic group (e.g., "pure Lao"), and "mixed," for those who identified with two or more ethnic groups (e.g., "mixed Vietnamese Chinese"). The majority of self-identified multiethnic teens had Chinese as part of the equation. This usually meant one of two things: they were Chinese but their families immigrated from a Southeast Asian country, or they were ethnically mixed Chinese (e.g., one parent was ethnic Chinese; the other was ethnic Cambodian), and their families immigrated from a Southeast Asian country. For the teens who identified simply as Chinese, this usually meant the former. Finally, there were also several teens throughout the years who identified as pure or mixed Lao and Vietnamese.

In contrast to how the teens most commonly identified themselves—primarily as Asian or ethnically as, for example, Lao or mixed Chinese Cambodian—throughout this book I frequently add American (e.g., Asian American, Vietnamese Chinese American) to their self-identification. This is largely a political move on my part, given that adding American to a racial or ethnic label can symbolize a claim to an American identity and an identification with the Asian American movement in the 1960s and 1970s (cf. Espiritu, 1992). Though the teens did not always see themselves as American or as political, I feel that it is my responsibility as an author to represent people of Asian descent in the United States as also American to not feed into the forever foreigner stereotype. I also use Southeast Asian American (a label they rarely used) or Other Asian (Sokla's label for Southeast Asian refugees) when emphasizing differences between the teens and other Asian American groups. When identifying individual teens throughout this book, I use their self-identified ethnic identity plus American in parentheses following their name.

Although the target population was Southeast Asian American youth, the video-making project in its last 2 years (2001–2002) began attracting teenagers from different Asian ethnic groups and even different racial groups. After the 1st project year, the video-making project was advertised simply as an after-school program, partly because the project organizers did not want to exclude Asian American teenagers who were not of Southeast Asian descent and partly because opening it up to all Asian Americans would ensure a large enrollment. There were no explicit rules that prevented non-Asian Americans from participating in the video-making project. In the final project year, the first Asian Americans who were not Southeast Asian joined the video-making project: Choi and Eva (Korean American females). Choi and Eva were invited by Asian Arts Initiative staff members, who did a recruitment presentation for the video-making project at Choi and Eva's high school in 2002. In the 3rd project year, the first non-Asian, Jill (Haitian Cuban American female), joined the video-making project. Jill was invited by her best friend Anh (Vietnamese Cambodian Chinese American female), who also joined the video-making project in 2001. By the final project year, there were a total of three non-Asian participants: Jill, Fred (European American male), and Rebecca (European American female), who went by Akiko, a Japanese name, because of her fascination and involvement with Japanese culture. Fred and Akiko, who attended the same recruitment presentation as their close friends Choi and Eva, joined the video-making project because of their interests in Asian culture and in video making. The presence of non-Southeast Asians at the video-making project brought about interesting tensions as well as opportunities for the teens to learn more about others and themselves. This book explores some of these issues, particularly with regard to how Jill and Choi influenced the construction of Asian American identities and stereotypes.

Discourse Analysis: Language, Identity, and Stereotype

The teenagers, though roughly 10 years younger, didn't seem too many worlds away from the innovative grassroots organizers who were making this exciting project happen. In the 1st project year especially, the adults connected extremely well with the teens, and the teens freely opened up about their lives to the adults. The other project organizers and I even attended parties that the teens were hosting; celebrated with them at local Cambodian festivals; invited them over for dinner; went to movies and restaurants together; and took road trips with them to conferences and film festivals in New York and Washington, DC. Over the years, the changing roster of adult volunteers—all of whom were Asian American though primarily not Southeast Asian American—generally upheld this tradition of developing meaningful relationships with the teen participants. In many ways, the video-making project was an ideal place to listen to the many voices and stories of Southeast Asian American youth, young people who had few safe spaces where they could talk openly about their lives, experiences, and perspectives.

With this overall atmosphere of open communication, project sessions usually ran smoothly as teens talked extensively about issues important to them, debated about Asian American images in mainstream media, and discussed how to construct their own representations as they created the stories, scripts, and characters for their videos. Most days were centered around lengthy and lively conversations, which I audio- or video-recorded on a regular basis. As I reviewed these tapes and reflected on the time I spent in the setting, I slowly came to realize that stereotypes were constantly being discussed, and discussed in surprising ways. I expected that a place like a video-making project would be filled with conversations about stereotypes—such as the forever foreigner stereotype, Asian martial-arts expert stereotype, and Asian storeowner stereotype—because the teen participants were in the process of creating their own media images of themselves in a distinctly Asian American organization. But I did not expect that the teen participants would sometimes believe these stereotypes, apply them to their lives, laugh about them, reproduce them in their videos, create new stereotypes, and even call each other "chink." Because many scholars in Asian American studies argue that stereotypes are homogenizing representations used by the dominant majority to oppress Asian Americans and other minorities (e.g., Hamamoto, 1994; R. Lee, 1999; S. Lee, 1996; Marchetti, 1993), I became a bit confused by what I was seeing: Asian Americans stereotyping themselves.

Because ethnographers attend to what participants themselves identify as important, I realized that I needed to closely examine these conversations about stereotypes to discover how the Asian American youth used them to construct a sense of who they were. Believing that identities are not stable but constantly emerging and changing through interaction (e.g., M. Goodwin, 1990; Hall, 1990), I decided to apply systematic tools of discourse analysis, methods that forced me to consider how these Southeast Asian American youth locally constructed stereotypes and their identities relative to them. Though on the surface these teens sometimes appeared to be simply reproducing stereotypes, through close discourse analysis I discovered that they were doing something much more complex and creative: Stereotypes became intricate and flexible tools with which to fashion their identities and relationships with others. Although a stereotype may be understood as an essentializing and oppressive representation, I argue that its locally achieved meaning can sometimes become more important to participants as they accomplish the immediate goals in an interaction. I am not suggesting that these teens were capable of transforming the meaning of stereotypes on a wider scale; however, I do argue that it is important to investigate the local ways in which people define and use stereotypes in everyday interactions if researchers are to understand how participants perceive and construct their identities.

Throughout this book, then, I use a linguistic anthropological approach to discourse analysis to examine how Southeast Asian American youth in an after-school program explicitly or implicitly constructed their identities in relation to stereotypes. Several other researchers used discourse analysis to explore youth identities in educational settings (e.g., Bailey, 2002; Bucholtz, 1997; Heath, 1983; Rampton, 1995a; Rymes, 2001; Wortham, 1994) and were extremely successful in producing compelling works that reveal new areas of knowledge that are otherwise missed by more conventional studies. This is because the analysis of interaction provides a fertile means to explore the complex organization of communities and to examine the manner in which identities form and develop through linguistic patterns in interaction. Although a considerable amount of discourse analytic research has been done with Latino and African American youth, Asian Americans have rarely been studied (but see, e.g., Chun, 2001; He, 2001; Lo, 1999; Lo & Reyes, 2004; Reyes, 2002). This book is among the forerunners examining Asian American discourse practices.

When conducting detailed discourse analysis, I use principled theories and methods that originated in literary theory, sociology, semiotics, and other disciplines and are embraced and developed by the linguistic anthropology of education (Wortham & Rymes, 2003). The roots of this discipline trace back several decades to researchers (e.g., Heath, 1983; Hymes, 1974; Philips, 1972) who were concerned with "studying linguistic patterns in use, searching for the native's point of view, and trying to connect micro- and macro-level processes" (Wortham, 2003, p. 4). Recently, as concepts such as indexicality and voicing have been further developed in linguistic anthropology, researchers examining youth in educational settings have focused increasingly on the close analysis of interaction by applying these concepts to transcripts of talk (Wortham, 2001, 2003). In the chapters that follow, I elaborate more on these and other concepts as they are applied in the analysis of discourse.

The Four Videos

Throughout the following chapters, I primarily analyze interactions that occurred during the weekly sessions at the video-making project. Each of the 4 project years yielded one 15-min video. In this section, I provide a brief synopsis of each of the four teen-created videos to give a general idea of the content, characters, and story lines that the teens devised with the assistance of adult volunteers and staff members. Told from the youth perspective, the videos primarily focus on issues that specifically concern Asian American communities. The videos have been shown at numerous schools, universities, community organizations, museums, conferences, small movie theaters, and film festivals in Philadelphia, New York City, and Washington, DC.

The first video, *American Sroksrei* (1999) (*sroksrei* is Khmer for "rice paddy"), centers on the lives of three fictional Southeast Asian American teenagers: Rocc, who recently left his gang and stopped using drugs to focus on his graffiti artwork and relationship with his straight-laced girlfriend; Buffy, Rocc's girlfriend and aspiring poet who does not like that Rocc is still friends with his old gang members; and Azeil, an independent spirit after Buffy's heart, who sees gangs as unnecessary and finds strength instead in hip hop and break dancing.

249 (2000) is a portrait of a single Cambodian immigrant father raising his teenage daughter and son. Perhaps the most somber of all the videos, this video tells the story of a family's struggles with intergenerational tensions and gender roles as the father wrestles with his alcoholism, which led his wife to abandon him and their children. As the father attempts to discipline his son for using drugs and his daughter for having a romantic relationship, he faces yet another challenge when his children decide to run away from home.

The third video, *Ba. Bay. Three.* (2001) (*ba* is Vietnamese for "three," and *bay* is Khmer for "three"), deals mainly with interethnic prejudice among Southeast Asian Americans. Moi is a Cambodian American teenage girl who begins dating Hoa, who is Vietnamese American. Driven by their prejudice against the Vietnamese, Moi's mother and brother forbid her from continuing her romantic relationship with Hoa. Conflicted, Moi must choose between her family and her boyfriend.

Finally, *These Are the Days* (2002) (whose footage was shot but has yet to be edited as of 2006), discusses the role peer pressure plays in romantic relationships. This video has the least specificity to Asian Americans, perhaps because in this final project year there were three non-Asian participants as opposed to previous years, which had only Asian Americans (1999, 2000) or only one non-Asian (2001). The story describes a more general high school experience with gossip, an ex-girlfriend, friends, and enemies, all playing a role in the demise of a teenage romance.

2

"No Kiss, No Money": Constructing Identities With Asian Newcomer Stereotypes

That's how Asian dads talk. He's F.O.B.

—Tommy, 2000

At a video-making project session in 2000, the meeting opened with an ice-breaker activity that involved the 16 Southeast Asian American teen participants and 6 Asian American adult volunteers (including me) with identity labels that we could not see taped to our backs. Almost every project session opened with an icebreaker, which was used to energize the group of teens at the start of each session, encourage interaction and group bonding among the teens and adults, and introduce the theme for the day in a stimulating and thought-provoking manner. The theme of the project session on this particular day was stereotypes and self-esteem. Mona (Filipino American female), an adult volunteer, planned the icebreaker, which was meant to confront participants with their own assumptions about how they apply stereotypes to others and how others apply stereotypes to them. We were instructed to walk around the room for 5 min and treat others like the identities taped to their backs, while trying to figure out our own identity. Afterward, Mona led a short discussion, asking us to reveal what people said to us, how it made us feel, and how we stereotype others based on labels. Among the labels used in the icebreaker were "Cambodian," "African American," and "White." As I walked around the room, the teens said to me "we cool," "yo what up," and "power to the people"; I had the African American label taped to my back. I also overheard some teens say "don't send me back" to the person labeled White, revealing a presupposition that European Americans

31

are in positions of power to decide whether or not to deport Asian immigrants, such as the 1.5 and second generation teens and their first generation parents.

Another identity label was "F.O.B.,"[1] a term that sparked a lively debate during the discussion portion of the icebreaker. Derived from "Fresh Off the Boat," F.O.B. is typically used derisively as a label for recently arrived Asian immigrants (cf. Jeon, 2001; Kang & Lo, 2004; Talmy, 2004). Moeun (Cambodian Chinese American male) was particularly vocal about his reported dislike for Asian newcomers during the discussion. On this and several other occasions, Moeun argued that Asian newcomers struggled but ultimately failed to integrate both linguistically and culturally into American society. Discussing the social and physical divisions at his high school, Moeun explained that Asian newcomers were isolated from the rest of the student body, relegated to "the second floor," where English as a second language classes and the Chinese bilingual education program were located. Repeatedly expressing frustration with the reported English language incompetence of Asian newcomers, Moeun once said, "F.O.B.s can't speak English, so they should just stop trying." He also ridiculed how Asian newcomers attempted unsuccessfully to style their hair and clothing according to current fashion trends.

I was perplexed by the amount of energy Moeun expended disparaging Asian newcomers, that is, until Moeun revealed to me that people sometimes called him F.O.B. Although the Southeast Asian American teens at the video-making project were all 1.5 and second generation, it hardly seemed possible to me that any of them could be considered Asian newcomers because they dressed, acted, and spoke in what seemed to be styles typical of urban youth culture. Yet considering the forever foreigner stereotype of Asian Americans, both foreign-born and American-born Asians fall prey to U.S. racial discourses that shape mainstream perceptions of Asian Americans as foreigners or recently arrived immigrants. Being identified as an Asian newcomer invited ridicule and contempt; thus, the more Moeun explicitly distanced himself from recently arrived Asian immigrants, the more he could avoid being located in the demeaning F.O.B. category.

---

[1]F.O.B. is pronounced as either an initialism (i.e., each letter pronounced individually) or an acronym (i.e., pronounced as a word). I use the spellings "F.O.B." for the former, and "fob" for the latter. Based on impressionistic data gathered from non-Asian and Asian American colleagues and friends, it appears that F.O.B. is more common on the East Coast, while fob is more common on the West Coast. The teens in this study typically used F.O.B. but sometimes used fob, especially in its derivative forms, for example "fobby" or "fobbish" (e.g., "fobbish voice").

But not all of the teenagers displayed the same perspective toward recently arrived Asian Americans. I assumed that the 1.5 generation teens in particular would express some empathy toward Asian newcomers because they also faced similar immigrant experiences, though usually at least a decade earlier. Yet sometimes 1.5 generation teens, like Moeun, were particularly critical of Asian newcomers perhaps because they were more at risk than second generation teens of being labeled F.O.B. For the most part, however, there was a mix of 1.5 and second generation teens who at times disparaged and at times defended Asian newcomers depending on conversational context. For example, in discussions about their parents, who were first generation immigrants and thus at risk of being labeled F.O.B., the teens often took a somewhat protective stance toward their families and other Asian newcomers. In discussions about themselves, some teens did not shy away from revealing facets of their lives that associated them with recently arrived Asian immigrants.

What the teens called "F.O.B. jobs" illustrates this latter point. The teens defined F.O.B. jobs in similar terms as sweatshop labor: work where employees, who are unprotected by labor unions and who are not required to understand English, undertake manual piecework for low pay. Several of the teens' parents reportedly worked such jobs, for example, assembling Christmas ornaments or sewing clothing in sweatshops in Chinatown, New Jersey, and other areas. The teens worked these jobs as well: For example, in the summers, Loc (Cambodian American male) picked blueberries in New Jersey, earning $3 for every large crate he filled; and during the school year, Enoy (Cambodian Chinese American female) assembled metal pieces in a factory. When Enoy was late for a party at the Asian Arts Initiative in 2001, she candidly announced, "My F.O.B. job kept me late." Enoy, as well as a few other teens, were often unafraid to admit that aspects of their lives connected them to Asian newcomers.

Sometimes these two perspectives—distancing oneself from Asian newcomers and associating oneself with Asian newcomers—met and brought about lively interactions, which assisted in the construction of youth identities. For example, in the quote that opens this chapter, Tommy (Cambodian American male) was defending the way he performed dialogue in the script of the 2001 video in which he played a Cambodian immigrant father. Moeun complained that Tommy was delivering his lines with an F.O.B. accent (nonnative English), but Tommy countered with a wider claim about the speech of their immigrant parents: "That's how Asian dads talk. He's F.O.B." While Tommy argued that his performance reflected the reality of how first generation Asian Americans speak, Moeun was adamant about not representing themselves and their families as Asian newcomers in their teen-created videos. The teens thus used stereotypes of recently arrived Asian immigrants to construct their own identities in divergent ways: While Tommy constructed an identity based on ideas of authenticity that linked his familial relations closely to the Asian newcomer stereotype, Moeun constructed an identity that distanced him from recently arrived immigrants by arguing that despite claims to reality, the stereotype should not be reproduced.

This chapter focuses on the multiplicity and complexity of these and other perspectives of the Southeast Asian American teenagers on the forever foreigner stereotype. I explore how the teens constructed their identities relative to stereotypes of Asian newcomers, particularly to stereotypes of Asian newcomer speech, what the teens locally called the F.O.B. accent, and what is known in the research literature as Mock Asian (Chun, 2004) or Stylized Asian English (Rampton, 1995a). In this chapter, I closely analyze discourse excerpts from an activity at a video-making project session in which the teens evaluated a popular film representation of a nonnative English- speaking Asian newcomer. Whereas some teens distanced themselves from the Asian newcomer portrayal, others authenticated Mock Asian as familial reality, and others used the depiction of the Asian newcomer and Mock Asian as evidence to critique White power structures for perpetuating the forever foreigner stereotype of Asian Americans in mainstream society. I then examine how nonnative English was scripted and performed in the teen-created videos as a representation of parental speech. The performance of Mock Asian potentially reproduced stereotypes of Asian newcomer speech, though within a system of opposition that provided a heterogeneous range of Asian American identities. The teens also used Mock Asian as a resource for constructing a complex sense of their families, lives, and identities while, however, still distancing themselves from recently arrived Asian immigrants.

IDEOLOGIES, INDEXES, AND STYLES OF THE ASIAN NEWCOMER

The forever foreigner stereotype of Asian Americans is embodied in a social persona that has been labeled in various ways. Although throughout this chapter

I use the terms "newcomer," "recently arrived immigrant," or "first generation" as labels for those who are often the prime targets of the forever foreigner stereotype, the teens did not. Instead they often used the label F.O.B., which, though largely an insult term, emerged with some complexity. Although I want to be clear that F.O.B. is not my term but the term that locally circulated among the teens at the video-making project, I nevertheless try to reveal the complicated ways in which the Southeast Asian American teenagers positioned themselves and their families relative to the forever foreigner stereotype through ideologies about the term F.O.B. and through one of the most salient indexes of the Asian newcomer identity: the Mock Asian linguistic style.

F.O.B.

Of the little scholarship on the label F.O.B., there is an agreement that ideologies about unacculturation and xenophobia are key elements in its meaning. Researching college students, Eble (1996) found that F.O.B. is a common slang term used to brand unassimilated Asian immigrants: "Asians who have not yet been acculturated to American ways are called F.O.B." (p. 121). Revealing how the term F.O.B. also emerges out of fear or dislike of foreignness, Eble (1996) claimed that "college student vocabulary about relationships echoes the discourse of American society at large. ... Increasing national fears about new immigrant groups are shown by *F.O.B.*" (p. 138). Similarly, Jeon (2001), in her ethnographic study of a Korean language college classroom in which she was also the instructor, further suggested that the term F.O.B. is directly related to its users' desire to keep Korean immigrants out of the United States and away from them and their families. She found that her students and their parents fear that through the continued admittance of Koreans into the United States, Korean Americans will be labeled F.O.B. if their peer group is entirely Korean immigrants or if they only speak Korean. Although primarily attempting to protect themselves from a type of discriminatory treatment often reserved for newcomers, minority groups at the same time can serve as conduits for larger hegemonic discourses by subscribing to assimilationist and xenophobic principles, which mainly serve the interests of the dominant White majority in the United States.

Both Jeon (2001) and Talmy (2004) also found that Asian and Pacific Islander Americans who are at risk of being labeled F.O.B. often deflect the label onto others as a strategy to avoid being labeled F.O.B. themselves. For example,

Jeon (2001) found that the term F.O.B. is used by her second generation students to differentiate themselves from what they perceive as unacculturated 1.5 or first generation Korean Americans. Just as Moeun was exceedingly vocal about his dislike for Asian newcomers above, one of Jeon's (2001) students stated, "F.O.B.s always hang out with other F.O.B.s, speaking only Korean to each other and acting like Koreans with Korean attitudes instead of acculturating into American society" (p. 98). Jeon (2001) found that for children in Korean immigrant families, English language proficiency and acculturation to American society must be accomplished first, and only after that is achieved can they feel comfortable exploring their Korean language and heritage. That is, once acculturated, an Asian American may feel less susceptible to being labeled F.O.B. and thus can move on to engaging in practices linked to Asian immigrants without fear of being labeled F.O.B.

Yet as long as the forever foreigner stereotype places Asian Americans at risk of being labeled F.O.B., Asian Americans will likely continue to be the most prominent users of the term. This is because the use of the label creates a division of Asian American identity that allows users to position themselves outside of the demeaning category partly by positioning other Asian Americans inside of it. In sum, at least three effects result from the use of the term F.O.B.: It locally redirects the insult term onto others, it upholds assimilationist values of the American melting pot, and it endorses discriminatory treatment toward immigrants and foreigners.

Mock Asian

According to the Southeast Asian American teenagers in the video-making project, there were several indexes of an F.O.B. or Asian newcomer. As stated earlier, some of these included physical markers, such as hair and clothing styles that fell short of complying with current fashion trends. But perhaps the most salient index of the Asian newcomer from the perspective of the teens was linguistic. The teens labeled Asian newcomer speech—a type of nonnative English linked to Asian immigrants—the "F.O.B. accent."

Although "accent" is not a precise term, sociolinguists and linguistic anthropologists have attempted to develop definitions. Rickford (1996), for example, stated that accent refers to "features of pronunciation alone—the phones, or individual sound segments in a word, as well as suprasegmental features like accent, tempo, and intonation" (p. 153). Exposing the myth of non-accent, Lippi-Green (1997) asserted the widespread sociolinguistic principle that both native speakers and nonnative speakers of a language have accents. For nonnative speakers, such as recently arrived immigrants to the United States, accent refers specifically to "the breakthrough of language phonology into the target language" (Lippi-Green, 1997, p. 43). Beyond linguistic considerations, Agha (2003) emphasized that "the folk-term 'accent' does not name a sound pattern as such but a system of contrastive social personae stereotypically linked to contrasts of sounds" (pp. 241–242). Accent is thus more than phonological features alone; it necessarily invokes a social schema that relationally situates particular categories of persons as linked to differential sound patterns. Only within such systems of distinction do accents gain meaning.

Recent work on style also engages with this idea of a system of distinction. The concept of style has been the subject of much sociolinguistic research, particularly in recent years (e.g., Bell, 1984; Coupland, 1985; Eckert & Rickford, 2001). Styles are ways of speaking; for example, dialects and registers can be considered styles. Yet Irvine (2001) emphasized that styles must be examined in a system of distinction. Specifically, she asserted that instead of being solely interested in the internal inventories of each particular linguistic style, researchers must investigate the principles of differentiation organizing the relationships and distinctiveness between styles. Styles only gain meaning within such systems of distinction where speakers and audiences play a role in creating and interpreting indexical links between languages and social groups. Ideologies also play an important role because they mediate the indexical links established between styles and categories of persons (e.g., Gal, 1998). Thus, for example, ideologies about unacculturation and xenophobia surrounding the Asian newcomer persona partly influence how indexical links become established between performances of a foreign accent and images of Asian Americans.

In this chapter, then, I am not interested in the actual speech of Asian newcomers but in the ways in which it emerges as a style that is performed and evaluated in relation to other categories of speech and persons. Instead of using the folk term "F.O.B. accent" or merely "accent," I follow Chun (2004) and use the term "Mock Asian" to describe stylized performances of Asian newcomer speech. Research on mock styles, for example, Mock Spanish (Hill, 1995) and Mock Ebonics (Ronkin & Karn, 1999), runs somewhat parallel to work on "language crossing," a term introduced by Rampton (1995a), who examined cross-racial use of Panjabi, Stylized Asian English, and Creole by multiethnic adolescent peer groups in England. Perhaps one of the main differences drawn between mocking and crossing concerns the effects: Although they both characterize performances of speech that is not straightforwardly linked to the speaker, mock language, to a large extent, has been described as relying on a certain type of dual indexicality (Ochs, 1990), which "overtly signifies speakers' desirable qualities ... [while] covertly 'inferiorizing' the language and culture of an outgroup" (Ronkin & Karn, 1999, p. 361). Whereas, in Rampton's (1995a) work, crossing into Stylized Asian English might partly qualify as mocking (because performances could reflect positively on the speaker and negatively on newly arrived South Asians), crossing into Creole largely did not (because performances could reflect positively both on the speaker and Afro-Caribbeans).

Whereas "Spanish" and "Ebonics" are terms for languages or linguistic varieties, there is no language called Asian; rather the term Mock Asian "emphasize[s] the racializing nature of this stereotypical discourse" (Chun, 2004, p. 263). Such widespread performances of Mock Asian partly function to help maintain the forever foreigner stereotype of Asian Americans by promoting an ideological link between a category of persons (Asian Americans) and a category of speech (nonnative English). Asian Americans as nonnative English speakers are then set within a system of distinction that positions them in contrast to other categories of persons (e.g., European Americans, African Americans), which can be linked to other categories of speech—for example, mainstream American English (MAE) and African American Vernacular English (AAVE). Although the honorary White stereotype may link some Asian Americans more closely to European Americans (and perhaps MAE) and the problem minority stereotype may link some Asian Americans more closely to African Americans (and perhaps AAVE), I argue that the pervasiveness of the forever foreigner stereotype and of Mock Asian across multiple sectors of American society dominates the folk perception of Asian Americans as primarily nonnative English speakers.[2]

---

[2]See Fig. 1.3 in chapter 1, which illustrates how the forever foreigner stereotype of Asian Americans underlies both the honorary White and problem minority stereotypes. That is, although the honorary White and problem minority stereotypes are set in opposition to one another, the forever foreigner stereotype can coexist with the perception of Asian Americans as both model and problem minorities.

Circulating across numerous arenas of American social life, Mock Asian has been historically established as a highly recognizable social practice. For example, Mock Asian can be found in film (e.g., a string of non-Asian actors, beginning with Warner Oland, portraying the character Charlie Chan in the 1930s and 1940s), television (e.g., the non-Asian actor Alex Borstein's character of Miss Swan on the weekly late-night comedy showcase *Mad TV* in the 1990s and 2000s), stand-up comedy (e.g., the contemporary Korean American comic Dr. Ken's impersonation of his immigrant father), as well as apparel (e.g., a T-shirt by Abercrombie & Fitch, a popular American clothing company, that reads: "Wong Brother's Laundry Service: Two Wongs can make it white" in 2002; see Chun, 2004). This last example illustrates a widely circulating stereotypical feature of Mock Asian: neutralization of /r/ and /w/ phonemes (e.g., "two Wongs can make it white" is a phonological play on the phrase "two wrongs can make it right": "wrong" [ɹɔŋ] → [wɔŋ]; "right" [ɹajt] → [wajt]).[3] Other salient linguistic features of Mock Asian include neutralization of /r/ and /l/ phonemes (e.g., "very" [vɛɹi] → [vɛri]); schwa epenthesis to closed syllables (e.g., "love" [lʌv] → [lʌvə]); and absence of articles (e.g., "pushing ø lawn mowing machine"). Although there are several other phonological, syntactic, lexical, and discourse features of Mock Asian (see Chun, 2004, for an extensive catalogue), I do not list them all here but instead highlight them as they appear in the data that follow.

ASIAN NEWCOMER PORTRAYALS IN MAINSTREAM FILM

As noted earlier, among the emblems of the Asian newcomer identity, nonnative English was perhaps the most salient index from the perspective of the Asian American teenagers at the video-making project. During my formal and informal interviews with them, I asked what they thought were the most prevalent Asian American stereotypes on television, in film, and at school. Two of the most popular responses were Mock Asian and the martial arts stereotypes. Although both stereotypes coincide with the forever foreigner stereotype of Asian Americans, the teens argued that the stereotypes positioned Asian Americans in

---

[3]See appendix for transcription conventions and chart of phonetic symbols.

disparate ways. Chea (Cambodian Vietnamese Chinese American male), for example, stated that Mock Asian produced an emasculated image of Asian American men since nonnative English suggested both social incompetence and bumbling deference (cf. Rampton, 1995a). In contrast, he argued that the martial arts stereotype was partly valuable because it presented an image of Asian Americans, particularly males, as strong and formidable. These two stereotypes are commonly found in media depictions of Asian Americans, and I turn now to a specific discussion of the representation of Asian newcomers, and particularly Mock Asian, in mainstream film.

This section analyzes discourse excerpts from an activity at the video-making project in 1999 in which the Asian American teenagers watched film representations of Asians and Asian Americans. The project session was designed by two adult volunteers, Mona (Filipino American female) and myself (Filipino European American female). Together, we created an activity that we hoped would accomplish two objectives: address the theme of the day, Asian American identity, which was a topic of interest selected by the teens weeks earlier, and provide an opportunity to view film representations of Asian Americans and follow the viewings with critical discussion, which might inform how the teens decide to represent themselves in their own teen-created videos. In the activity, the teens viewed four short clips from the following films: *Supercop* (Tong, 1992), *Wayne's World* (Spheeris, 1992), *Sixteen Candles* (Hughes, 1984), and *Mulan* (Bancroft & Cook, 1998). The activity was designed with a group of three judges and three other groups, each consisting of an adult volunteer and four or five teen participants. After watching each clip, groups gathered privately for 2 min to discuss both the positive and negative aspects of the portrayal. Each group then reported to the whole group one thing that was positive, one thing that was negative, and whether the representation was more positive or negative overall. Groups who matched the judges' decision won points.

Mock Asian in *Sixteen Candles* (1984)

The excerpts that I analyze in the following section occurred after the teen participants viewed a film clip from a popular teen movie from the 1980s, *Sixteen Candles*. The film features Gedde Watanabe, a Japanese American actor in his first major role, portraying the character of Long Duk Dong, an exchange student from China. Watanabe is a monolingual American English speaker who was born and raised in Utah; he claims that his performances of Asian-accented English are informed by how his older relatives speak (Lim, 2001). In the film, Long Duk Dong is staying with the grandparents of the main character, Samantha (Sam), who is European American. In the clip that was shown to the teens, the grandparents who are hosting Long Duk Dong, Howard and Dorothy, and Sam's other set of grandparents, Fred and Helen, are guests in Sam's home in an Illinois suburb, having dinner in the dining room with Sam and her younger brother, Mike.

The scene opens with the sound of a gong followed by plinky-plunky "Chinese" music. Long Duk Dong slowly raises his head (as if from a bow) from the dining room table after tasting his food, which he is eating using his silverware as chopsticks. The family members at the table gaze at Long Duk Dong, as if anxiously awaiting his reaction to the meal. Long Duk Dong then speaks in a soft, breathy, monotone voice with slow tempo and lexically timed rhythm. He comments that the dinner is "clever" and "interesting" because it fits into a "round pie." Mike tells him that it's a quiche. Long Duk Dong asks how it is spelled, and one of the grandparents, Fred, tells him that you don't spell it, you eat it, which is followed by laughter. A few moments later, Long Duk Dong tells everyone how he enjoys visiting "grandma" (Dorothy) and "grandpa" (Howard), writing letters to his parents in China, and mowing the lawn for Howard so that his "hyena" is not disturbed. Mike corrects him by saying "hernia," which is followed by laughter. At the end of the scene, Dorothy asks Sam if she will take Long Duk Dong to the high school dance with her. As a look of horror and disgust appears across Sam's face, another gong is sounded.

Throughout the scene are several features of Mock Asian in the speech of the Chinese newcomer character Long Duk Dong. Set in opposition to the relatively uniform MAE spoken by the European American characters, Long Duk Dong's speech emerges contrastively with a decreased tempo, softer pitch, and choppy rhythm, timed primarily to words and sometimes syllables. In addition to these suprasegmental features, there are phonological and syntactic features of Mock Asian (some of which are also general features of nonnative or nonstandard English) in Long Duk Dong's speech. In terms of phonology, Mock Asian features include neutralization of /r/ and /l/ (e.g., "clever" [klɛvəɹ] → [krɛvə]; "interesting" [ɪntɹəstɪŋ] → [ɪntɛɾestɪŋə]); coda /r/- deletion (e.g., "dinner" [dɪnəɹ] → [dɪnə]); schwa epenthesis to closed syllables (e.g., "fit" [fɪt] →

[fitə]; "with" [wɪθ] → [wɪθə]; "and" [ænd] → [ændə]); trilled /r/ (e.g., "round" [ɹaʊnd] → [raʊnd]); [ə] → non-reduced vowel (e.g., "grandma" [gɹændmə] → [grændmɑ]); and increased aspiration (e.g., "grandpa" [gɹændpə] → [grændpʰɑ]). In terms of syntax, Mock Asian features include absence of articles (e.g., "appetizing food fit neatly into ø interesting round pie") and absence of third-person present tense (e.g., "food fit neatly"; "hyena don't get disturbed").

Although some of these Mock Asian features can also be features of other nonstandard varieties, for example, AAVE (e.g., absence of third-person present tense), I argue that such ambiguity still privileges an interpretation of these features as Mock Asian. This is because the linguistic features co-occur with several other nonnative linguistic features in Long Duk Dong's speech as well as with several nonnative, nonlinguistic features of Long Duk Dong's portrayal, for example, his unfamiliarity with Western eating utensils and food items and the sounds of Eastern music that bookend the scene. The emergent opposition between the suprasegmental, phonological, and syntactic features of the speech of the European Americans and of the Chinese newcomer accentuate Long Duk Dong as Other (Said, 1978), not only along linguistic lines but along several other axes of identity, including race, national origin, and culture.

The Asian Newcomer Film Portrayal Within an Indexical Field

As the Southeast Asian American teenagers discussed the portrayal of Long Duk Dong, they drew on indexical resources that functioned to situate the teens close to or far from the Asian newcomer identity. In Peirce's (1932) semiotic framework, unlike icons that resemble their objects or symbols that are analogous to their objects indexicals have a spatiotemporal connection with what they refer to or, more generally, an existential relation with their referents (Burks, 1948). Indexicals are signs, such as pronouns or gestures, that cue both text-internal cotextual relationships (what is said before and after) and text-external contextual relationships (aspects of the situation) (Silverstein, 1998). Indexical forms thus rely on both surrounding cotext and context for their meaningfulness, while making salient particular aspects of cotext and context (Benveniste, 1954/1971; Peirce, 1932; Silverstein, 1976).

In the excerpts that follow, the teens make significant use of both nonpro-nominal indexicals, such as "people" and "the man," as well as pronominal in-dexicals, mainly first- and third-person pronouns, as they evaluate the Asian newcomer portrayal. Third person is unlike first or second person in that it does not correspond to any specific participant role in the speech event (Lyons, 1977). In her study of how prisoners narrate stories about stabbing their victims, O'Connor (1994) found that shifting between first person to impersonal "you"—while still indexing the self—distances the speaker from the act of stab-bing. In the following analysis, the teens performed a similar move by indexing Asian newcomers with both first-person pronouns (thus identifying as Asian newcomers) and third-person pronouns (thus not identifying as Asian newcom-ers, who are instead framed as absent from the speech event). Although O'Connor (1994) noted that a shift from "I" to "you" is an act of distancing by the speaker, I argue that shifts from "we" to "they" mark a type of distancing as well.

The following excerpt begins after the teens watched the clip from *Sixteen Candles*. Mona, who was the moderator for this activity, instructed us to con-verse privately in our respective groups for 2 min. The following excerpt is of the group of judges: me (Angie), Loc (Cambodian American male), and Ny (Vietnamese Lao Cambodian American female). Rather than provide my opin-ions, my role in the group of judges was to facilitate the task by making sure Loc and Ny reached a mutual decision about whether the portrayal was more positive or negative overall.

(1)

```
1    Angie:   ok so, what
2    Ny:      because Asian person maybe can't speak right
3             and (?) and it could be a person right, like a
4             person's house you know, they want to take
5             care of him. I don't see nothing negative
6             about it
7    Angie:   why
8    Loc:     'cause you know that Asian people- they be
9             trying to making- fun of us man just- just
10            cause we can't speak that well and stuff, the
11            man gotta try and make fun of us? and you know
12            they try and make stereotypes and stuff
```

```
13   Ny:      but the story is true it could be true
14   Loc:     look, hold up- hold up but I do agree with her
15            though, cause you know when I first came here-
16            y'know when my family first came here y'know
17            they didn't speak that well English either so
18            I agree with her (.) I go with her answer
19   Angie:   so then should we say it was positive? ok all
20            right, we're quick
```

The first thing mentioned about the depiction of Long Duk Dong is Mock Asian. Ny argues that it may be accurate in the world that there are several nonnative English-speaking Asians who struggle linguistically (line 2). She then claims that the grandparents take care of Long Duk Dong, which reflects favorably on Asian people (lines 4–6). Describing Long Duk Dong as a vulnerable newcomer who benefits from the care of European Americans, Ny states there is "nothing negative" (line 5) about the representation because, according to her, the representation is both accurate and favorable. Ny thus "authenticates" (Bucholtz & Hall, 2003) the portrayal of the Asian newcomer, including the performance of Mock Asian, based on claims to reality.

Loc, then, draws on pronominal indexicals, such as "we" and "they," to discuss the source of Asian newcomer representations and the impact they have on Asian Americans. Loc begins his argument with a nonpronominal indexical, "Asian people" (line 8), then switches to "us" (line 9) and "we" (line 10), while the referent, "Asian people," appears to remain intact. By replacing "Asian people" with first-person plural pronouns, Loc simultaneously positions himself in the "Asian" category, thereby grouping himself with other Asian Americans. Although Loc agrees with Ny that it is accurate in the world that "we" Asians struggle with the English language (line 10), he argues that "they" were making fun of "us" (lines 8–9). Yet it is not entirely clear what group of people is indexed by the pronoun "they." For example, "they" could index the European American characters in the film or index an omnipotent "they" who control the widespread representations and stereotypes of Asian Americans, such as the producers of such Hollywood films as *Sixteen Candles*. When Loc says "the man" (lines 10–11), a cotextual relationship between "they" and "the man" begins to emerge. "The man" substitutes for "they," while the poetic structure (Jakobson, 1960) of the utterance remains largely intact: from "they be trying to making- fun of us" (lines 8–9) to "the man gotta try and make fun of us" (lines

10–11). This parallel suggests that "they" and "the man" index the same refer-ent. Thus, "they" comes to refer less to specific characters in the film and more to "the man," which is likely short for the White man (Chun, 2001, p. 54), a popular term used often by people of color to criticize institutional structures, such as the entertainment industry, which are disproportionably controlled by European Americans.

Ny retorts, "but the story is true" (line 13); then Loc concedes that the rep-resentation of the Asian newcomer speaking nonnative English is ultimately positive based on similar claims to authenticity or genuineness that were ex-pressed by Ny. But whereas Ny simply claims that aspects of the portrayal are "true," Loc roots his authentication of Mock Asian in a narrative about his fam-ily's immigration. Relating the Asian newcomer film portrayal to when his fam-ily first immigrated to the United States provides evidence for his change of opinion. Yet while he begins his story with first-person pronouns, he later shifts to third-person pronouns, which functions to gradually distance him from his narrated experience. Loc initially uses first-person singular, "I," in the utterance "when I first came here" (line 15) but then repairs this utterance midsentence by replacing "I" with "my family" while maintaining the poetic structure of the ut-terance: "when my family first came here" (line 16). Moving from "I" to "my family" in the telling of the immigration story places less emphasis on Loc and more emphasis on his family as immigrants. Loc then removes himself com-pletely from his narrative with a third-person pronoun: "they didn't speak that well English" (line 17). Although Loc's immigration narrative potentially posi-tions him as once inhabiting the Asian newcomer and Mock Asian stereotypes, Loc's indexical shifts—from "I" to "my family" to "they"—gradually distance him from the Asian newcomer persona. Thus, through indexical resources, Loc, on the one hand, positions his family ("they"), and not necessarily himself, as prior nonnative English-speaking newcomers, while, on the other hand, locating himself within a larger group of Asian Americans ("we," "us") who fall victim to stereotypes perpetuated by White power structures. That is, regardless of whether Asians speaking nonnative English is accurate in the world or not, Loc blames "the man" for perpetuating Mock Asian and the forever foreigner stereotype of Asian Americans.

The use of first- and third-person pronominal and nonpronominal indexicals in this excerpt begins to construct a discursive field within which groups emerge in relation to one another. Loc, through the use of first-person pronouns, "us," "we," "I," and "my family," both establishes a group of Asian Americans and locates himself within this group, which falls victim to a separate discursively constituted group, "they" and "the man," who are characterized as controlling how Asian Americans are represented. Ny and Loc use third-person indexicals for Asian Americans as well: "Asian person," "him," "Asian people," and "they." Thus, in the indexical field, European Americans emerge as a separate group of others in opposition to Asian newcomers, who are constructed as both a group of others and a group within which Loc, though not necessarily Ny, locates himself.

After the private small group discussions, Mona invited each group to share what they discussed with the whole group about the film representation of Long Duk Dong, with the judges reporting last. The following excerpt is from the first group that presented. They begin by echoing what both Ny and Loc discussed privately in the previous interaction.

(2)

```
21    Pen:    it's positive because it shows how other
22            people be nice to Asian people. see grandma
23            like the little kid. dig it, all right
24    Loc:    they was bustin' on us man
25    Pen:    ok negative 'cause see how they make the dude
26            talk. give him a strong accent … it's really
27            negative 'cause the strong accent
```

Pen (Cambodian American male) reports that his group discussed both Mock Asian and the treatment of Long Duk Dong. Pen first mentions that the portrayal is positive because the Asian newcomer character was treated kindly (lines 21–23). After Loc shouts out "they was bustin' on us man" (line 24), Pen comments on Mock Asian, specifically how "they make the dude talk" (lines 25–26). This indexical "they" seems to cue a cotextual relationships with Loc's "they" in the previous line as well as in the previous excerpt: That is, Pen contributes to the construction of an indexical field within which an omnipotent "they" is criticized and blamed for contributing to the maintenance of the forever foreigner stereotype in American society.

As the second group reports, Sokla (Cambodian American male) inserts an example from his immigrant history, just as Loc privately did earlier.

(3)

```
28   Sokla:   the reason it's positive right, why I thought
29            positive is that, this clearly is a guy right,
30            he was- he was clearly a person who came to
31            America not so long ago right, and he still
32            (?) with the language … that was really really
33            really be y'know a real a real … it could be
34            something that be true cause (?) I remember
35            when I came right, I act the same way too, I
36            mean no language y'know I just laughing and
37            they be laughing at me, yeah but the movie
38            right, I think the movie really did really
39            show a good good good example of Asian people
40            … like if you just came over and you didn't
41            know stuff like that
42   Moeun:   yeah but they bust on him though, it's like
43            naw
44   Sokla:   no no no no, that's not the point, our group
45            was saying was the guy, was the Asian guy
46            presented, was he stereotyped or not y'know …
47            I think, I think I would be the same way as a
48            person who just came over
```

Sokla agrees that the representation is partly positive based on Mock Asian being "real" (line 33) and "true" (line 34) of recently arrived Asian immigrants. He proceeds to tell an immigrant narrative, just as Loc did earlier, which again functions to authenticate the portrayal of the Asian newcomer and his use of Mock Asian. Sokla says, "I remember when I came right, I act the same way too, I mean no language y'know I just laughing and they be laughing at me" (lines 34–37). Sokla joins Loc and Pen in invoking "they" when discussing the poor treatment of Asian newcomers. Yet one key difference between the immigration narratives told by Loc and Sokla is that Sokla tells the entire story in first-person, unlike Loc, who gradually shifted from first person to third person midnarrative. By admitting that he was a recently arrived immigrant like Long Duk Dong, Sokla, unlike Loc, explicitly locates his past self as an Asian newcomer.

Following Loc, Pen, and Sokla, Moeun (Cambodian Chinese American male) continues to construct an indexical field centered around a third-person

"they." Moeun performs the same move that Loc did in the previous excerpt:
interrupt the person reporting to assert that "they" treat "him" (Long Duk Dong)
poorly (line 42). This relates cotextually to Pen's argument about how "they"
make "that dude" (Long Duk Dong) speak (lines 25–26). Yet whereas Moeun
and Pen construct an indexical field in which they are absent because there are
only third-person members ("they," "him," "the dude"), Loc and Sokla construct
an indexical field in which they are present because there are third-person
("them") as well as first-person members ("us," "I," "me," "my family").

After the members of the third group shared their opinions, which repeated
many of the same points that others made, the judges reported what they had
discussed to the entire group.

(4)

```
49   Loc:     like Moeun said y'know, they was bustin' on us
50            man, just cause we Asian and we can't talk
51            right they gotta bust on us? …
52   Ny:      I think that movie is like- true as people
53            could make fun of-
54   Sokla:   Asian people
55   Ny:      yeah they call us chinks gooks and stuff. I
56            think it's positive because it's like it's so
57            true, and we do- some people can't speak right
58            either, they have an accent too so I think
59            it's true
```

Although Moeun originally said "they bust on him" (line 42), Loc quotes Moeun
as having said "they was bustin' on us" (line 49). The replacement of
third-person "him" to first-person "us" reframes Moeun's utterance to match
Loc's "they was bustin' on us" (line 24), said moments earlier. Loc thus recruits
Moeun into the indexical field with him by reframing Moeun's utterance from
"him" to "us." Next, Ny reiterates what Loc suggested privately in our small
group, that the depiction is "true" (lines 52, 57, 59) because it reflects how
Asian Americans are ridiculed by others. Ny also authenticates Mock Asian
based on these same claims to genuineness (lines 57–59). Moreover, she offers
ethnic slurs, "chinks" and "gooks" (line 55) that "us" Asians are sometimes
called as evidence that "they" and "people" make fun of Asian Americans. Ny,
following Loc and Sokla, inserts herself into the indexical field through this use

of "us" (line 55). Yet as Loc did earlier, Ny begins with first-person "us" and "we," then shifts to third-person "some people" (line 57) and "they" (line 58), which functions to initially associate her with nonnative English-speaking Asian newcomers but then subsequently distance her from them.

These excerpts reveal the complex and shifting ways in which the Southeast Asian American teenagers evaluated and positioned themselves relative to the Asian newcomer portrayal in mainstream film. Fig. 2.1 represents how through the use of first- and third-person pronominal and nonpronominal forms, an indexical field within which groups emerged in relation to one another was established. The teens constructed two indexically differentiated groups of Asian Americans—third person ("Asian people," "they," etc.) and first person ("us," "I," etc.)—and set them in opposition to a separate discursively constituted group—third person ("they," "the man," etc.)—who were characterized as controlling how Asian Americans are represented. The teens differentially constructed their identities relative to the stereotypes of Asian newcomers and Mock Asian, sometimes within the same utterance.

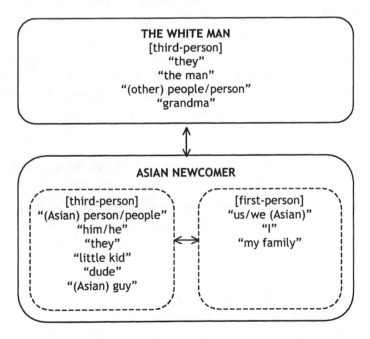

FIG. 2.1 Three contrastive personae within an emergent indexical field.

For example, Loc's and Ny's indexical shifts from first person to third person served to first associate them with the Asian newcomer persona as they authenticated the portrayal, then immediately distance them from it. In contrast to Loc and Ny, Sokla unequivocally embraced the Asian newcomer and Mock Asian film portrayal as an authenticated representation of who he once was as a recently arrived immigrant. Moeun and Pen, on the other hand, did not insert themselves into the indexical field; instead, their use of third-person indexicals to evaluate the Asian newcomer portrayal positioned them with a more detached stance. Yet Loc was able to recruit Moeun into the first-person indexical area when he reframed Moeun's stance from detached to involved with the pronoun "us." This fluidity with which Loc, Moeun, Ny, and others were able to move between indexing Asian newcomers with first- and third-person forms is represented by the dotted lines in Fig. 2.1. Finally, all teens—Loc, Pen, Moeun, Sokla, and Ny—used the portrayal of the Asian newcomer as evidence for their critique of "they" and "the man," who were accused of mistreating Asian Americans and perpetuating the forever foreigner and Mock Asian stereotypes.

By creating an indexical field, which primarily situated European Americans in opposition to two concepts of Asian Americans, the teens were able to both authenticate the Asian newcomer portrayal and critique institutional structures blamed for perpetuating it. At the same time, the teens were able to accomplish these moves without necessarily or decisively inserting themselves into the indexical field, which would have associated them with Asian newcomers, a social category they often scorned.

ASIAN NEWCOMER PORTRAYALS IN THE TEEN-CREATED VIDEOS

Even though most of the Southeast Asian American teenagers tended to be critical of how Asian Americans were often portrayed as nonnative English-speaking newcomers in mainstream media, it did not prevent them from depicting Asian newcomers and Mock Asian in their own teen-created videos. Although most of the characters in all four teen-created videos were young people modeled largely on the teens' own lives and perspectives, Cambodian immigrant parent characters appeared in videos *249* (2000) and *Ba. Bay. Three.* (2001). Though both videos portrayed Asian newcomers, only *Ba. Bay. Three.* portrayed Asian newcomer speech. Originally, the Cambodian immigrant father in *249* was supposed to speak Mock Asian, but a few teens, particularly Moeun (Cambodian Chinese American male), objected. As described at the opening of this chapter, Moeun criticized Tommy's (Cambodian American male) portrayal of the Cambodian immigrant father during a script reading for *249*. Although Tommy claimed that he was attempting to accurately represent how the parents of the Asian American teens speak, Moeun was able to convince the adult artists and volunteers as well as the other teen participants that Tommy should not use nonnative English in his portrayal of the character. Although Tommy ultimately portrayed the role of the Cambodian immigrant father with a mix of Khmer (Cambodian) and an AAVE-inspired variety, teens such as Anh (Vietnamese Cambodian Chinese American female) still labeled his performance fobbish because of nonlinguistic aspects of the depiction: For example, according to Anh, he spoke Khmer, expected his daughter—not his son—to do the housework, was an alcoholic, and wore a white tank top. Yet in the video the following year, *Ba. Bay. Three.*, Phila (Cambodian Chinese Indian American female) met no resistance as she portrayed the role of a Cambodian immigrant mother using Mock Asian.

In the teen-created videos, first generation Asian immigrant characters emerge in contrast to 1.5 and second generation Asian American characters, and Mock Asian emerges in contrast to other speech styles, such as MAE or AAVE. Positioning heterogeneous Asian American personae within such systems of opposition creates possibilities for constructing and dividing multiple Asian identities. As discussed in the previous section, indexical resources allowed the teens to divide the Asian newcomer category and to cross in and out of the Asian newcomer identity. In this section, a division of identity also solidifies, but one based primarily on intra-Asian intergenerational difference. Although the teens also drew on authentication to justify the reality or genuineness of Asian immigrant speech, I explore the extent to which the performances of Mock Asian in the teen-created videos potentially index and perpetuate the forever foreigner stereotype of Asian Americans. That is, I examine whether the Asian American teenagers were engaging in a practice for which mainstream film producers and "the man" were criticized: participating in the widespread circulation of Asian Americans as unacculturated immigrants.

Mock Asian in *Ba. Bay. Three.* (2001)

Ba. Bay. Three. focused on the forbidden interethnic relationship between Moi, a Cambodian American teenage girl, and a Vietnamese American teenage boy. There were several other young characters in the video with the exception of Mrs. Liu, Moi's mother, played by Phila. The following transcript is of a scene from the video in which Moi's mother enters the bedroom of Moi, played by Anh, as she is getting ready to go to a party.

(5)

```
60    Mother:  <speaking in creaky, monotone voice with
61             lexically timed rhythm> where are you going?
62                                          [wɛ]
63    Moi:     I'm going to a party with Em and Ny
64    Mother:  then why you so dressed. I- why you braid your
65                           [drɛst]              [brɛd] [jɔ]
66             hair like that?
67             [hɛ]       [dæt]
68    Moi:     'cause it's the new style
69                                    [staju]
70    Mother:  you and your style. (hh) you're so concerned.
71                 [jɔ]    [staju]              [kənsən]
72             (1.14) what- why are you wearing silver, I
73                                   [wɛriŋ]   [sɪlvə]
74             told you- how come you not wear the gold I buy
75             you?
76    Moi:     'cause the silver look better with what I'm
77             wearing
78    Mother:  better, (0.5) that's what you're always
79             [bɛtə]            [dæts]
80             concerned with, aren't you.
81    Moi:     yes::
```

There are several features of Mock Asian in the speech of the Cambodian immigrant mother portrayed by Phila. Set in opposition to the daughter's largely MAE variety, the mother's speech emerges contrastively as monotonal and creaky with a choppy rhythm. In addition to these suprasegmental features, there are several phonological and syntactic features of Mock Asian in the mother's speech. In terms of phonology, Mock Asian features include trilled /r/ (e.g., lines 64–65: "dressed" [dɹɛst] → [drɛst]; "braid" [bɹed] → [bred]); coda /r/- deletion (e.g., lines 61–62: "where" [wɛɹ] → [wɛ]; lines 64–67: "your hair" [jɔɹ hɛɹ] → [jɔ hɛ]; lines 72–73: "silver" [silvɚɹ] → [silvə]); coda /l/- deletion (e.g., lines 70–71: "style" [stajl] → [staju]); neutralization of /r/ (e.g., lines 72–73: "wearing" [wɛɹɪŋ] → [wɛrɪŋ]); absence of flapping (e.g., lines 78–79: "better" [bɛrɚɹ] → [bɛtə]); alveolarization of interdentals (e.g., lines 66–67: "that" [ðæt] → [dæt]); and consonant cluster simplification (e.g., lines 70–71: "concerned" [kənsɚɹnd] → [kənsən]). A syntactic feature of Mock Asian in the mother's speech is auxiliary ellipsis (e.g., line 64: "why ø you so dressed"; line 74: "how come you ø not wear"). Although some of these may also be features of other nonstandard varieties of English, I argue that their co-occurrence within a pattern of nonnative forms privileges the interpretation of her style as Mock Asian.

The Asian Newcomer Video Portrayal Within a System of Opposition

Phila's performance of Mock Asian in her portrayal of a Cambodian immigrant mother is informed by the widely circulating and thus highly recognizable stereotype of the Asian newcomer. This image gains part of its meaning by how it emerges relationally to other social categories in play. Irvine (2001) points out:

> Images of persons considered typical of those groups—and the personalities, moods, behavior, activities, and settings, characteristically associated with them—are rationalized and organized in a cultural/ideological system, so that those images become available as a frame of reference within which speakers create performances and within which audiences interpret them. This system informs the style-switching in which all speakers engage. To put this another way: one of the many methods people have for differentiating situations and

displaying attitudes is to draw on (or carefully avoid) the "voices" of others, or
what they assume those voices to be. (p. 31)

Performing Mock Asian, Phila draws on the available "voice" (Bakhtin,
1935/1981) of the Asian newcomer or forever foreigner stereotype, which helps
create a recognizable portrayal of a Cambodian immigrant mother. There are
principles of differentiation that organize the field of opposition that emerges
between this voice and the voice of social others, namely, the daughter, Moi.
Thus, an analysis of Mock Asian without regard to how it is set in a system of
distinction with other categories of speech and personae is incomplete.

Set in contrast to the mother's speech, the daughter's speech is largely an
MAE variety incorporating some nonstandard features: for example, coda /l/-
deletion (e.g., lines 68–69: "style" [stajl] → [staju]) and absence of third-person
present tense (line 76: "the silver look better"). Though coda /l/- deletion and
absence of third-person present tense are features of both nonstandard and nonnative English, they likely emerge here as features of a nonstandard—not nonnative—variety, perhaps an AAVE-inspired style. This is because the ambiguous features do not co-occur within a pattern of Mock Asian features in Moi's
speech but rather within a pattern of nonstandard features commonly attributed
to AAVE. Moi's AAVE-inspired linguistic features are frequently heard elsewhere in the video: for example, slang terms, such as "aite" (all right) and "yo,"
and syntactic features, such as subject-verb disagreement ("I didn't know you
was in the bathroom") and multiple negation ("I can't do nothing"). Moreover,
Moi's corn-row-braided hairstyle and her fondness for hip hop music (revealed
in a different scene) are also inspired by African American urban youth cultural
styles. Recursivity (Gal, 1998) thus characterizes the emergent opposition between Moi and her Cambodian immigrant mother as it operates along multiple
linguistic and nonlinguistic levels (e.g., AAVE-inspired MAE vs. Mock Asian;
child vs. parent; silver vs. gold; corn rows vs. no corn rows). This system of distinction begins to divide the category of Asian American by presenting competing images of Asian Americans.

The following excerpt is a continuation of the scene between Moi and her
mother:

(6)

```
82   Mother:  look at me. <Moi quickly glances at Mother>
83            (1.2) now I want you to tell me the truth
84                                                [truθ]
85   Moi:     (2.4) about what
86   Mother:  do you have a boyfriend?
87                              [bɔjfrɛn]
88   Moi:     no: (0.5)
89   Mother:  Moi (1.6)
90   Moi:     yes? (1.5)
91   Mother:  are you honest?
92                      [ɑnɛs]
93   Moi:     ye:s, you taught me better. [I wouldn't lie-
94   Mother:                              [I taught you
95            better but how many times have you
96            disappointed me
97   Moi:     m::: once?
98   Mother:  once? (1.0) how about once every week?
99                                        [ɛri]
100  Moi:     uh uh::: once.
101  Mother:  uh uh. that's your favorite expression every
102                                      [ɛksprɛʃən]
103           time you do something wrong (1.1)
104                              [rɔŋ]
105  Moi:     no::
106  Mother:  hh you used to be a good girl you know
107  Moi:     I'm still a good girl
108  Mother:  then how come you- <Moi takes out lipstick>
109           (2.5) s- s- stop- p- put that down, you don't
110           need makeup.
111  Moi:     okay
112  Mother:  how come you s- (.) you stop talking to me
113  Moi:     'cause I'm busy, I don't have time
114  Mother:  you don't have [time for family
115  Moi:                    [I got- I gotta go
```

Phila continues to draw on Mock Asian features in her portrayal of the Cambodian immigrant mother. Most salient are her continued use of trilled /r/ (e.g., lines 83–84: "truth" [tɹuθ] → [truθ]; lines 101–102: "expression" [ɛkspɹɛʃən] → [ɛkspɹɛʃən]; lines 103–104: "wrong" [ɹɔŋ] → [rɔŋ]), consonant cluster simplification (e.g., lines 86–87: "boyfriend" [bɔjfɹɛn] → [bɔjfrɛn]; lines 91–92: "honest" [ɑnɛst] → [ɑnɛs]), and a combination of both (e.g., lines 98–99: "every" [ɛvɹi] → [ɛri]).

The division between opposing Asian American identities continues to solidify not only through the principle of style differentiation (i.e., Mock Asian vs. AAVE-inspired MAE) but also with regard to other aspects of the two portrayals. I noted earlier how nonlinguistic differences between the two Asian American characters emerged with respect to, for example, kin relations (child vs. parent) and hairstyle (corn rows vs. no corn rows). Whereas the mother continues to be cast along the image of a traditional immigrant parent, particularly with regard to her use of Mock Asian, the daughter continues to be cast along the image of a problem child: disapproval of her hairstyle (lines 64–66) and the accusations regarding her romantic relations (line 86), dishonesty (line 91), repeated disappointments (line 96), and disobedience (line 103). According to her mother, Moi is no longer the "good girl" (line 106) she used to be.

In the following scene, Moi and her mother engage in another interaction but one that is quite different from the two earlier excerpts. Unlike in the previous scene in which the emergent recognizable identities of Moi as delinquent child and her mother as traditional parent were invoked for their performance, here Anh draws on another recognizable identity for Moi, that of obedient daughter. Prior to the later scene, Moi finally admitted that she had a Vietnamese boyfriend to her mother, who then gave Moi an ultimatum: choose between her boyfriend and her family. The viewer does not know what Moi decided to do before the following interaction in which Moi approaches her mother, who is washing dishes in the kitchen.

(7)

```
116  Moi:     mommy::
117  Mother:  hmm?
118  Moi:     can I get moneys to go to the movies with Ny
119           and Em?
120  Mother:  hold on. <turns off faucet, dries hands> (7.4)
121           what do you want?
```

```
122  Moi:     I want- ten dollars to go with Ny and Em to
123           the movies
124  Mother:  ten dollars?
125              [dɑlɑ]
126  Moi:     no fifteen dollars <smiles>
127  Mother:  fifteen dollars?
128              [dɑlɑ]
129  Moi:     yeah <smiles more widely, tilts head to side>
130  Mother:  (girl) give me kiss first
131              [gi]      [ki]   [fəs]
132  Moi:     o:::h (wh-) (na::::) <whining>
133  Mother:  give me a kiss first, no kiss no money
134              [gi]      [ki]   [fəs]      [ki]
135  Moi:     fine m::a:: <kisses Mother with exaggerated
136           kissing sound> give me fifteen
137  Mother:  hmn.
138  Moi:     mom (it's) only ten
139  Mother:  I didn't like your kiss <smiles and gently
140                          [jɔ]  [ki]
141           pats Moi's hand>
142  Moi:     <giggles> bye mom
143  Mother:  (bye)
```

Again, Phila and Anh draw on contrastive styles in the performance of their characters. Phila continues to draw on Mock Asian features in the portrayal of the mother. Most notably, she uses coda /r/-, /z/-, and /v/- deletions (e.g., lines 124–125: "dollars" [dɑləɹz] → [dɑlɑ]; lines 130–131: "give" [gɪv] → [gi]; lines 139–140: "your" [jɔɹ] → [jɔ]) and consonant cluster simplification (e.g., lines 130–131: "first" [fəɹst] → [fəs]); and [ɪ] → [i] (e.g., lines 130–131: "kiss" [kɪs] → [ki]). Anh, on the other hand, while continuing to draw primarily on MAE, begins using a child's register with her use of lexical items, such as "mommy::" (line 116), whinelike elongations, such as "o:::h" (line 132), wide grins (line 129), docile head tilts (line 129), an exaggerated kissing sound (lines 135–136), and childlike giggling (line 142). Unlike the previous scene in which the mother approached Moi and proceeded to accuse her of improper behavior, here Moi, who no longer wears corn-rowed braids in her hair, approaches her mother for a favor. Both Moi and her mother display affection toward one another with smiles, kisses, and physical contact.

Fig. 2.2 positions these three emergent and contrastive representations within a system of opposition: problem child, good girl, and strict parent. The depth and complexity with which Moi in particular was portrayed moved beyond the flat and homogeneous images of Asian Americans commonly found in mainstream media. For example, while Moi was being cast as a delinquent child in the first two excerpts, in other parts of the video she was portrayed as an academically oriented obedient daughter; she was often studying for exams, writing papers, and explicitly expressing how she did not want to disappoint her parents by performing poorly in school. These competing sides of Moi's character merged to provide a more multifaceted, hybrid portrayal rather than an either-or depiction of identity, which is represented by the permeable dotted lines that separate these two personae in Fig. 2.2.

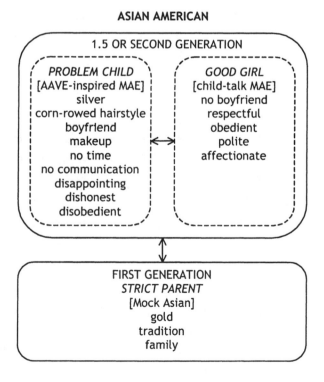

FIG. 2.2 Three contrastive personae within an emergent system of opposition.

Although in the last scene Moi was being cast as an obedient daughter, it was soon revealed that her behavior was only a pretense; she was leaving the house not to go to the movies with her girlfriends Ny and Em but rather to meet her Vietnamese boyfriend. Moi chose to deal with her mother's ultimatum by leading a dual life where she could, on the one hand, be true to herself by continuing her romantic relationship and, on the other hand, please her family, though with a false sense of who she was. Moi's pensive glance in her mother's direction as she left the house to meet her boyfriend reflected her conflicted feelings, which only seemed to add to the complexity of Moi's character.

Although Moi's character was drawn with rich and intricate strokes, she as well as the other teen characters remained in stark contrast to the foreigner stereotype, which was occupied by the first generation character alone. Thus, the teens were able to portray the Asian newcomer without identifying as the Asian newcomer, a social category that the teens often authenticated yet deflected onto others.

Perhaps given that the videos were created by 1.5 and second generation Asian American youth, and not by first generation adults, the characters based on the teens' lives tended to emerge with more complexity than those based on their parents. Moi's mother, for instance, was presented in a more static fashion than Moi herself: Throughout the video, the mother remained stern, traditional, and unyielding, but at the same time she was a powerful character with emotional depth, unlike many mainstream Asian depictions, such as Long Duk Dong. Yet regardless of the extent to which the teen-created Asian newcomer character was depicted flatly, that it emerged within a system of opposition that positioned this Asian American persona in relation to several others still served to counteract the dominant media representations of Asian Americans as a largely homogeneous group of unacculturated immigrants. That is, although "the man" and the teen videographers potentially recirculated the forever foreigner stereotype through the Asian newcomer depictions of Long Duk Dong and Moi's mother, respectively, that Long Duk Dong was the only Asian newcomer portrayal while Moi's mother emerged among several Asian American portrayals proved to be a key issue: It is not only the depth of the depiction itself but how the depiction emerges within a system of opposing depictions.

CONCLUSION

This chapter reveals the multiple and complex ways in which the forever foreigner stereotype interacted with how the Southeast Asian American teenagers constructed a sense of who they and their families were. Nonnative speech emerged as the most salient index of the Asian newcomer persona because the teens often focused on Mock Asian in their evaluations and performances of recently arrived Asian immigrants. Ideologies of unacculturation and xenophobia partly informed how the teens tended to distance themselves from the Asian newcomer persona often by deflecting the identity onto others through, for example, the use of derisive labels such as F.O.B. Despite largely resenting the circulation of the forever foreigner stereotype in mainstream media, the teens tended to authenticate depictions of recently arrived Asian immigrants as familial reality, allowing them to justify the recirculation of Asian newcomer portrayals in their own teen-created videos.

By attending closely to the discourse surrounding Asian newcomer stereotypes, this chapter examined the often subtle and intricate uses of language in the construction of indexical fields and systems of opposition that positioned the Asian newcomer persona relative to youth identities. In both the evaluations of Asian newcomer characters in mainstream media and the performances of Asian newcomer characters in the teen-created videos, the Southeast Asian American teenagers built fluid models that allowed them to traverse multiple available personae in the momentary construction of their identities. Some teens, for example, grouped themselves with Asian newcomers by indexing them with first-person pronouns (e.g., "we") as quickly as they disaligned themselves from Asian newcomers by referring to them with third-person pronouns (e.g., "they"). While White power structures were locally indexed as a major presence in the making of mainstream depictions of Asian Americans, they were absent in the making of the teen-created videos. Instead, at the video-making project the portrayals were controlled by the teens, who seized the opportunity to create complex media representations of their own lives. These portrayals were set in contrast to the forever foreigner stereotype, which was reserved for the construction of the characters based on their first generation parents.

Although several teens criticized "the man" for portraying Asian Americans as foreigners in mainstream film, they still reproduced a similar Asian newcomer image in their own videos. Yet whereas *Sixteen Candles* (1984) presented a single, flat, and homogeneous foreigner depiction of Asian Americans, the teen-created video, *Ba. Bay. Three.* (2001), produced a similar portrayal but in conjunction with an array of multiple and complex Asian American characters. The after-school video-making project allowed the Asian American teens to take control of their own representations, as they created both rich and diverse Asian American portrayals as products of their identities. In the next chapter, I take a close look at how a different stereotype influenced the types of identities that the teens constructed for themselves. Whereas this chapter focused on the influence of the forever foreigner stereotype, the next chapter explores how the problem minority stereotype was used in the making of youth identity.

3

"Aite" and "Na Mean":
Constructing Identities
With African American Stereotypes

All Asian kids want to be Black.

—Moeun, 2000

If the newcomer identity was primarily associated with the past for the Southeast Asian American teenagers, African American identity was often associated with their present and future. According to the segmented assimilation model by Portes and Zhou (1993), rather than assimilating to the dominant White majority in the United States, several teens were traveling the second trajectory: acculturation to socially and economically marginalized minority communities. Like many immigrant minorities settling in poor, urban areas across the United States, most of the teens in this study identified more with the experiences of low-income African Americans than with those of the White mainstream. Because their neighborhoods and schools, though multiethnic, were predominantly African American, the Asian American teens had more contact with African Americans than with European Americans. Although most of their friendship groups consisted of other Southeast Asian Americans, many teens also had close African American friends, who frequently accompanied them to the video-making project and other events at the Asian Arts Initiative.

Teens like Moeun (Cambodian Chinese American male), Narun (Thai Cambodian Chinese American female), Anh (Vietnamese Cambodian Chinese American female) and Jill (Haitian Cuban American female) even accused their Asian American peers of "acting Black" because of how they dressed, talked, and behaved. Participating heavily in hip hop culture, the vast majority of teens

62

wore clothing, accessories, makeup and hairstyles popular among African American youth, and many of the male teens practiced break dancing, graffiti art, record spinning, rapping, and R&B singing at the video-making project and in their neighborhoods.

Though consumed with commodities and practices associated with African American youth culture, the teens did not directly reproduce these forms; instead they often reshaped them with a distinctly Asian or Asian American quality. For example, Leroy (Cambodian Chinese American male), who enjoyed hip hop music, wrote a rap song, "Me a Cambo, You a Pinay," about his interethnic relationship with a Filipina American. The teens also relished in the aspects of Asian culture that were the object of fascination of many African Americans (cf. Prashad, 2002), such as the Wu-Tang Clan, a popular rap group named after kung fu fighters at the Shaolin Temple, the subject of many Chinese martial arts films in the 1970s. The male teens frequently rented these films and drew graffiti of the Shaolin Temple, incorporating kung fu fighters and Chinese dragons into their designs. Through these hybrid practices, the teens were not simply following the second trajectory of assimilation to African American identities but incorporating the third acculturation trajectory posited by Portes and Zhou (1993): the deliberate preservation of and conscious solidarity with cultural practices, values, and beliefs linked to the immigrant community.

Language is also central to this issue of hybrid segmented acculturation. Not only did the teens embrace social practices linked to African Americans in the formation of their identities, but they also incorporated linguistic features linked to African Americans in their displays of speech. As these Asian American youth constructed who they were along an identity trajectory that moved from newcomer to urban minority, a parallel speech trajectory emerged that coupled newcomer identities with nonnative English, on the one hand, and urban minority identities with African American Vernacular English (AAVE), on the other. This movement from Asian-accented speech to AAVE-influenced speech parallels the movement from Asian English to Creole for Panjabi youth in Britain. Rampton (1995b) finds that "Asian English conjured a past that Panjabi adolescents now felt that they were leaving behind" (p. 505), oftentimes in favor of Creole, which was frequently referred to as the "future language" (p. 506). Like Creole, AAVE has emerged as an influential language, given its authority in the global culture of hip hop.

The Asian American teens in this study were also subject to this influence, as many displayed AAVE features in some of their speech at least some of the time. In discourse excerpts taken from Reyes (2002, 2004) and from this chapter, the teens produced the following linguistic features often said to be characteristic of AAVE: copula ellipsis (e.g., "yo yo he Cambo"; "it like"; "you still Philly"; "they coming up"); absence of third-person present tense (e.g., "he know how to protect himself"; "he try to come"; "she look kinda aite"); and negative concord (e.g., "they don't know nothing"; "you don't got no problem"). Although it may be the case that a few teens spoke AAVE systematically, it is more accurate to characterize the speech of the majority of the teens as a hybrid variety that frequently incorporated features of AAVE as well as features of Vietnamese, Khmer (Cambodian), Lao, or other home languages of the teens.

In much of second language acquisition research, there is an assumption that the target language for second language learners is the standard variety. Many scholars challenge this assumption by investigating the possible and multiple target language varieties and reference groups of language learners (e.g., Beebe, 1985; Eisenstein, 1982; Zuengler, 1989). As with the case of Panjabi youth favoring Creole or of Southeast Asian refugee youth favoring AAVE, deviations from standard forms may not be errors of second language learners; rather, they may reflect their choice of target varieties and reference groups (Ellis, 1994).

Focusing on the concept of reference group, Goldstein (1987) examined the preferred target variety of 28 advanced Latino English as a second language students from urban high schools in New York. She found a correlation between the amount of reported contact with African Americans and the presence of AAVE grammatical features in their speech; however, reported identification with African Americans proved to be insignificant. Although most of the Asian American teens in this study lived in African American neighborhoods and identified with African American social practices, some teens had more peer contact with African Americans than with others. It might follow that those with more direct contact with African Americans would speak AAVE features more systematically, whereas those without direct contact would not. Yet rather than analyze the systematicity of AAVE features in the speech of the teens, and then link these results to their reference groups, I am more interested in how the teens understood AAVE features, constructed their use of them as "authentic" or not, and used these features in the production of their identities.

Unlike the previous chapter on the forever foreigner stereotype, this chapter explores how the problem minority stereotype affected the lives of the Southeast Asian American teenagers. Focusing on one aspect of AAVE, I examine the ways in which the Asian American teens constructed and used African American slang as an interactional resource to position themselves and each other relative to stereotypes of African Americans. Whereas some teens racialized certain slang terms as belonging to African Americans, other teens authenticated identities as speakers of African American slang. Through close analysis of slang-in-use and particularly of the metapragmatic discussions such uses inspired, this chapter explores how the teens specified relationships between language, race, age, region, and class. Focusing on two African American slang terms, I examine the ways in which the teens appropriated slang for multiple social purposes, such as identifying with African Americans, perpetuating stereotypes of African Americans, marking urban youth subcultural participation, and interactionally positioning themselves and others as teachers and students of slang. Emerging with local linguistic capital, slang was used by the teens to create boundaries not only between teens and adults but also between each other. I argue that the discursive salience of region implicitly indexed socioeconomic status and proximity to African Americans as markers that the teens drew on to authenticate themselves and others as slang speakers.

CROSS-RACIAL USE OF AFRICAN AMERICAN LINGUISTIC STYLES

Labov's (1972) seminal work, *Language and the Inner City: Studies in Black English Vernacular*, brought the study of African American speech practices to the center of sociolinguistic inquiry. Although this speech variety has been referred to by different names over the past several decades, I use the term African American Vernacular English (AAVE), which is also preferred by many current scholars of AAVE. Much AAVE research has been dedicated to AAVE's complex histories, structures, uses, and politics (e.g., Baugh, 1983, 1999, 2000; Kochman, 1981; Mitchell-Kernan, 1972; Mufwene, Rickford, Bailey, & Baugh, 1998; Rickford & Rickford, 2000; Smitherman, 1977, 2000), making AAVE one of the most-studied varieties of American English. The central argument of this work is that AAVE is not "bad" English; rather, AAVE has its own rule-governed linguistic system consisting of phonological, morphological, syntactic, and discourse features. Although varieties of Latino English have also been widely studied along similar models of AAVE research (e.g., Fought, 2003; Metcalf, 1979; Peñalosa, 1980; Penfield & Ornstein-Galicia, 1985; Ryan, 1979), the language practices of Asian Americans have disrupted dominant sociolinguistic paradigms that presume a kind of one-to-one mapping between a linguistically distinct form of English and a racially distinct group (Reyes & Lo, 2004). Although evidence for an Asian American English akin to AAVE or Latino English has generally been inconclusive (e.g., Hanna, 1997; Mendoza-Denton & Iwai, 1993; Spencer, 1950; Wolfram, Christian, & Hatfield, 1986), this does not prevent Asian Americans from drawing on available linguistic resources to construct their identities in discursive practice. Yet borrowing linguistic resources to do identity work inevitably raises sensitive issues, particularly when speakers cross racially defined linguistic lines to do so.

The question of how Asian Americans use AAVE features in the construction of their identities engages the issue of "styling the other" (Rampton, 1999; see also Rampton, 1995a, on language crossing), which is concerned with the "ways in which people use language and dialect in discursive practice to appropriate, explore, reproduce or challenge influential images and stereotypes of groups that they don't themselves (straightforwardly) belong to" (Rampton, 1999, p. 421). Many scholars argue that such styling practices across racial groups are bound with complex tensions involving racialization and appropriation (e.g., Hewitt, 1982; Rampton, 1995a). Whereas racialization involves linking a way of speaking to a distinct racial formation, appropriation entails crossing into the linguistic variety that has been formulated as that of the racial other and exploiting it for new uses and effects. These twin processes can be found in Le Page and Tabouret-Keller's (1985) discussion of the use of London Jamaican by non-Jamaicans in England. Developing an argot as a result of discrimination in the host society and as a symbol of solidarity, London Jamaicans as a group gain prestige among young people, yet "the prestige is transferred to the argot itself, which is then adopted by those who do not possess the stigmatized physical features but nevertheless wish in some way to identify with the group" (p. 246). Non-Blacks then benefit through appropriating locally prestigious language forms from a stigmatized race without becoming stigmatized themselves.

In seeming contrast to racialization and appropriation, the concept of authentication can be used to examine the ways in which linguistic styles are discursively constituted as one's own "authentic" speech. As part of Bucholtz and Hall's (2003) tactics of intersubjectivity model, through which language and identity can be examined, authentication refers to the processes by which people actively construct an identity based on ideas of genuineness or credibility. The practices of cross-racial users of AAVE, for example, who formulate AAVE as their own variety exhibit this process of authentication. In this chapter, I consider how processes of racialization, appropriation, and authentication are integral in examining the ways in which speakers actively construct their identities through discursively constituted links between speech varieties and categories of persons.

There has been some work on European Americans crossing into AAVE (e.g., Bucholtz, 1997, 1999; Cutler, 1999; Hatala, 1976; Labov, 1980; Sweetland, 2002), but even less exists on AAVE use by Asian Americans (but see Bucholtz, 2004; Chun, 2001; Lo, 1999; Reyes, 2002). Whereas some European American users of AAVE are met with suspicion because they are not accepted as legitimate AAVE speakers (e.g., Bucholtz, 1997, 1999; Cutler, 1999), others can be authenticated as AAVE speakers within local speech communities (e.g., Sweetland, 2002). Though authenticated use of AAVE by Asian Americans has yet to be documented, its occurrence is not unlikely. However, instead of passing as fluent AAVE speakers or trying to "act Black," many Asian Americans use AAVE features to lay claim to participation in an urban youth style (e.g., Bucholtz, 2004; Chun, 2001), much like most European Americans who use the variety (e.g., Bucholtz, 1997; Cutler, 1999).

As for Asians in the diaspora outside of the United States crossing into Black speech styles, Rampton's (1995a) work remains a seminal account of the social meanings achieved when Asian immigrants cross into Creole, which is spoken primarily by Afro-Caribbean immigrants in England. Because youth admired Creole, which "stood for an excitement and excellence in vernacular youth culture" (Rampton, 1995b, p. 506), Rampton argued that such crossing practices are an example of uni-directional double-voicing (Bakhtin, 1929/1984), where self and voice, or principal and figure (Goffman, 1981), are intertwined. This close entanglement between the speakers (Panjabi youth) and what they spoke (Creole) signaled favorable evaluations of Creole. Though Asian immigrants are not the main focus of Hewitt (1986), he similarly found that because of the prestige of British Jamaican Creole, "Asian teenage boys were occasionally members of black friendship groups and used creole with their black friends. Black youth culture was apparently felt to be so attractive an option for some Asian boys that they even artificially curled their hair, wore Rasta colours and attempted to 'pass' for black" (p. 195). Both Hewitt (1986) and Rampton (1995a) found that as is also common in the United States, many Asian immigrants associate with Black youth culture, creating closer ties between Asian and Black identities through language and other semiotic means.

African American Slang

Although AAVE consists of several linguistic features, this chapter focuses on one aspect of AAVE: African American slang. At this juncture, it is important to highlight two points: (1) Slang is a component of AAVE (as it is a component of several other language varieties), but it is only a small part of the vocabulary of AAVE (Green, 2004), and (2) while not all slang is of African American origin, African Americans have contributed enormously to American English slang (Eble, 1996). Yet researchers have found that people often reduce AAVE to slang (e.g., Sweetland, 2002), and some of the teens in this study were no exception. As shown in this chapter, several teens used the term "slang" to describe only African American slang and not other types of slang from other language varieties. They often equated the terms "AAVE" and "slang" (among others, such as "ghetto" and "Ebonics"), which served to reduce AAVE to merely slang, while simultaneously racializing the term "slang" as African American speech.

Many scholars argue that slang terms rooted in African American culture, such as "cool," "hip," and "gig," are taken up by mainstream Americans because nonmainstream lifestyle and speech are seen as inventive, exciting, and even alluringly dangerous (Chapman, 1986). Eble (2004) notes, "Adopting the vocabulary of a non-mainstream culture is a way of sharing vicariously in the plusses of that culture without having to experience the minuses associated with it" (p. 383). Much like the situation of cross-racial use of AAVE, while non-African Americans may gain local social prestige by peppering their speech with African American slang terms, they do so without suffering the daily experiences with discrimination that plague the lives of many African Americans.

Bucholtz (in press) argued that very little scholarly work has examined how slang is used cross-racially: Although there has been some work examining the use of African American slang by European Americans, studies of its use by Asian Americans are extremely scarce. Analyzing how Asian Americans adopt

African American slang brings a fresh perspective to this body of research because, unlike European Americans, Asian Americans share racial minority status with African Americans. Yet unlike other minority groups, Asian Americans are uniquely positioned by contradicting U.S. racial ideologies, which, although still largely operating along a Black-White racial dichotomy, have managed to carve out positions for Asian Americans as forever foreigners and honorary Whites. A third stereotype has emerged that positions some Asian American groups—particularly Southeast Asian refugee youth—as problem minorities who have fallen prey to stereotypes traditionally assigned to African Americans. Unlike middle-class European American youth, the low-income Southeast Asian American teens in this study were positioned more closely to the African American experience based on a shared socioeconomic and minority status. Asian American cross-racial—though not cross-minority—use of African American slang provides new perspectives on the various discursive practices available to non-Whites as they establish their identities relative to African American linguistic styles.

METAPRAGMATICS AND INDEXICALITY OF SLANG-IN-USE

Eble (1996) describes slang as "an ever changing set of colloquial words and phrases that speakers use to establish or reinforce social identity or cohesiveness within a group or with a trend or fashion in society at large" (p. 11). Because nonmainstream culture and music are particularly influential in setting trends, young people, especially, adopt slang created by African Americans who dominate the entertainment world (Chapman, 1986). Because slang is associated with signaling coolness and engagement in youth culture, it has also been viewed as signifying resistance to established structures of power. Sledd (1965), for example, stated that "[t]o use slang is to *deny allegiance* to the existing order" (p. 699). Yet slang does not always mark resistance, nor does such resistance always manifest itself in a binary division between society and anti-society (Halliday, 1976). Using slang to divide youth identities is oftentimes more important to adolescents than using slang to separate youth subcultures from the dominant mainstream (Bucholtz, in press).

Although slang is commonly understood as ephemeral and informal vocabulary, researchers have focused more on identifying slang by its effects, rather than by its form or meanings (Eble, 2004). Given this focus on communicative effect, which is contingent on multiple contextual factors in any interactional instance of slang use, there is no precise formula for knowing if a particular term or phrase qualifies as slang. Thus, rather than marking a clear lexical territory, slang describes a fluid range of words and expressions that locates its users within a social terrain. Similar to how the concept of style has been approached by many sociolinguists (e.g., Bell, 1984; Coupland, 1985, 2001; Eckert & Rickford, 2001), slang should not be defined by its internal inventory but by how principles of differentiation organize the relationships and distinctiveness between slang and its alternatives (cf. Irvine, 2001). This chapter is thus primarily concerned with how slang emerges within a contrastive system of discursive options and produces various social meanings and effects linked to issues of race, appropriation, and authentication.

Although work on slang has emerged over the past few decades, only a small number of studies moved beyond methodological approaches that rely almost exclusively on questionnaires and elicited definitions of slang terms. Yet the process of construing the meaning of slang should be less focused on the actual slang terms, and more focused on how slang emerges in interaction. By relying on reports of slang use rather than analyzing slang-in-use, researchers may be accessing ideologies of slang but not the practices of slang (Bucholtz, in press). As researchers move the interactional details of slang-in-use to the center of inquiry, they may discover implicit discursive strategies that construct additional meanings and functions of slang that are missed by more traditional approaches that rely solely on slang definitions at face value.

Such examinations of how slang emerges in interactions can access native metapragmatic stereotypes about slang (Agha, 1998). That is, researchers can examine interactional details to discover the stereotypes that are invoked and linked to the use of slang in particular interactional contexts. These stereotypes emerge through denotationally explicit and implicit metapragmatic evaluations (Silverstein, 1976, 1993). That is, sometimes the stereotypes are stated explicitly by interactants, and sometimes they are accomplished implicitly through linguistic patterns that veil the subtle meanings and evaluations that participants construct for slang.

To decipher the metapragmatics of slang, researchers can analyze the indexical patterns in an interaction. Although the literal meaning of a slang term is somewhat stable, its indexical value is not nearly as fixed. The referential value of the slang term "cool," for example, is "good," an adjective that indicates a positive assessment of some entity or practice. How the use of "cool" is indexical of a type of personhood that is set in social and cultural relation to the speaker and audience, however, is indecipherable without appeal to the situation of utterance. Like pronominal indexicals, such as "they" and "we," whose meanings are reliant on their occasion of use, slang terms also rely partly on surrounding context for their meaningfulness, while making salient particular aspects of context (Benveniste, 1954/1971; Peirce, 1932; Silverstein, 1976). That is, while uttering "cool" is partly shaped by the context—for example, an informal setting may foster an atmosphere where "cool" is said frequently—uttering "cool" can also shape the context—for example, saying "cool" in a formal setting may make the situation less formal. Moreover, while uttering "cool" can signal participation in youth culture when used casually by a teenager, it can conversely signal exclusion from youth culture when used awkwardly by an adult.

Thus, slang can achieve multiple meanings and effects depending on contextual factors, such as who utters it, who is listening, what the situation is, what the purpose is, and so on. In this chapter, I analyze how the Asian American teens use African American slang, a practice through which indexical links may run wild, possibly functioning to reproduce, challenge, or redefine the social and interactional meanings of slang. Coupling ethnographic data of participant perspectives with the close analysis of indexical patterns in interactions, I examine the implicit meanings and effects that are most likely achieved through the use of slang.

TWO AFRICAN AMERICAN SLANG TERMS: "AITE" AND "NA MEAN"

Through a combination of phonological and morphological processes, the phrases "all right" and "do you know what I mean?" produce, respectively, the slang word and phrase, "aite" and "na mean."[1] In conjunction with phonological modifications, word blending forms "aite" [aˑiʔt] (also spelled, e.g., "aight,"

---

[1] These spellings conform to the ways in which the teens most often spelled these slang terms in the scripts of the teen-created videos.

"aiight," the latter iconically orthographizing vowel lengthening), and word blending and clipping form "na mean" [nɑːmiʔn] or [njɑːmiʔn] (also spelled, e.g., "nya mean," "nameen"). Similar to the various functions of the expressions "all right" and "do you know what I mean?" in mainstream American English (MAE), "aite" was often used by the teens as an adjective (e.g., "she look kinda aite"), and both "aite" and "na mean" were frequently used as discourse markers (Schiffrin, 1987) drawing interactants into seemingly shared meanings and stances by, for example, seeking agreement, comprehension, or attention (e.g., "I got this idea, aite?"; "it's just run down, na mean?"). "Aite" and "na mean" are commonly recognized as having emerged from African American culture in the past decade or so and are often still considered to be spoken primarily by African Americans. Yet any potential racial marking of these slang expressions relies less on their pragmatic function and more on their phonetic contour and contextual placement, as is shown later.

I argue that "aite" and "na mean" are slang terms—and not simply phonological variants or pragmatic particles—because they constitute alternatives to the conventional expressions "all right" and "do you know what I mean?" That is, "aite" and "na mean" are often deliberately chosen to send social signals: for example, to convey an informal or flippant attitude or to identify with a trend or social group. A similar logic supports the view of "diss"—"disrespect"—as a slang expression as well: Though some might argue that "diss"—as well as "aite" and "na mean"—are merely clipped words, Eble (2004) recognizes "diss" as a slang term because of its social force.

Over all 4 years of the video-making project, several teens frequently used "aite" and "na mean," among other African American slang terms. Anh (Vietnamese Cambodian Chinese American female), Sokla and Bao (Cambodian American males), for example, regularly said "aite" and "na mean" in everyday interaction. There were some teens, however, who rarely used these slang terms. These teens typically lived in predominantly White, middle-class neighborhoods on the outskirts of urban Philadelphia. Anh, Sokla, Bao, and several others who habitually used "aite" and "na mean" resided in poor neighborhoods in South Philadelphia with large African American populations.

Yet often Anh's, Sokla's, and Bao's performances of African American slang were linguistically marked. For example, as Sokla was preparing to appear on camera moments before a video shoot, he repeated "na mean" numerous times before the camera rolled, as if he needed to practice his delivery of this slang phrase. Likewise, Anh sometimes paused before she said "na mean," and a few times Anh said "all right, aite" as if repairing "all right" by immediately following it with "aite." These teens may have been deliberately trying to use African American slang and thus deliberately trying to display a self-image that linked them more closely to African American culture or urban youth identity. Thus African American-inspired youth culture emerged with local prestige as many teens admired and aspired to it through their linguistic choices, as well as through their music, clothing, and other lifestyle practices.

RACIALIZATION OF SLANG

Examining discourse and ethnographic data that reveal the ideologies and practices of slang, these next few sections analyze how the teens racialized African American slang and authenticated identities as speakers of African American slang. This first discourse excerpt from a project session of the video-making project in 2002 reveals how the Asian American teens directly linked slang to ghettoness, and later racialized the use of slang as "Black" speech. The teens displayed varying proficiencies in African American slang, and in this excerpt Macy (Vietnamese American female) was trying to teach Will (Chinese American male) how to say "na mean." Anh (Vietnamese Cambodian Chinese American female) and Van (Vietnamese American female) also entered the conversation.

(1)

```
1    Macy:    say na mean (.) Will [come on
2    Van:                          [I can't talk slang
3    Macy:    you can't?
4    Will:    what's slang
5    Anh:     [slang
6    Macy:    [sla::ng
7    Will:    oh what's slang oh- oh sla::ng
8    Van:     except if I'm really mad
9    Will:    [na mean (.) na mean
10   Macy:    [hmm hmm hmm the ghettoness comes out
11   Van:     heh heh yes heh heh
```

In this interaction, slang becomes metapragmatically equated with anger and ghettoness, and a social boundary based on slang competency is constructed to set Van and Will apart from Macy and Anh. Van, who "can't talk slang" (lines 203) and Will, who asks "what's slang?" (line 5), stand in contrast to both Macy, who models "na mean" for Will (line 1), and Anh, who responds in unison with Macy by repeating the word "slang" (line 6) as if in disbelief that Will does not even know the term. Van goes on to say that she can speak slang but only if she is "really mad" (line 8). Macy, then, explicitly links speaking slang to "ghettoness" (line 10) which, like "na mean," is another slang term popularized by African American culture.[2]

Dual Indexicality

Two weeks later, I asked Van what she meant when she said she only spoke slang when she is angry. Van said that when she is angry, she wants to be more "scary" or "mean." She then made the following comment:

(2)

```
12    Van:    it makes me feel ˚Black˚, or at least South
13            Philly
```

Taking excerpts (1) and (2) together, slang becomes discursively linked to being mad, ghetto, Black, and South Philly. Van lowered her voice to a whisper when she said the word "Black" to me, which might mark that Van did not want to be overheard, as if it was embarrassing or wrong to say. Yet not only did Van racialize slang as belonging to African Americans, but she also regionalized it as South Philadelphia speech. Van, who did not live in South Philadelphia, linked slang to this area, which was largely African American. Her explicit reference to

---

[2]Although "ghetto" is believed to have been derived from the Italian word "borghetto" and used in the 17th century to indicate parts of cities where Jewish people were restricted, in the late 19th century it was appropriated in the United States to indicate crowded urban areas populated by ethnic minorities. Today, it has become redefined again by African American culture to indicate lifestyle, places, speech, dress, people, and other entities that possess a quality akin to an urban, lower socioeconomic, and generally tacky sensibility. For example, some teens note that there are "ghetto schools," "ghetto friends," and "ghetto neighborhoods."

South Philadelphia elucidates that it was place of residence—and also class and race—that distinguished the two groups of teens: African American slang incompetent Van and Will, who lived in middle-class neighborhoods on the outskirts of Philadelphia, and African American slang competent Macy and Anh, who lived in poor and working-class neighborhoods in South Philadelphia.

That slang made Van "feel Black" reveals how her racialization and appropriation of slang relied on dual indexicality (Hill, 1995; Ochs, 1990). By using African American slang to directly index herself as tough, Van reaped the benefits of the stereotype of the aggressive African American portrayed in popular culture as violent, criminal, and deviant (Ronkin & Karn, 1999; van Dijk, 1987). Although Van may have drawn on the stereotype of violence out of admiration, she also indirectly indexed African Americans negatively by reproducing the stereotype. Van profited from the effects of her racialized linguistic resource as she appropriated the local social capital linked to an imagined formidable and hostile African American from South Philadelphia. Yet although the linguistic appropriation allowed her to construct a tough identity for herself, it did not require Van to experience any other aspects of being African American that are lived every day (Smitherman, 2000). Although such language crossing practices allow speakers to transgress fluid linguistic, ethnic, and cultural boundaries, Van revealed how these practices can also reinforce social hierarchies and racial ideologies in everyday interaction (Rampton, 1999).

Triple Indexicality

Through racializing and appropriating slang, Van relied on dual indexicality, whereas other teens, I argue, relied on triple indexicality not only to reflect positively on the borrower and negatively on the borrowee but also to construct alliances between Asian Americans and African Americans. Chun (2001), in her study of Jin, a Korean American male who uses imagined AAVE and African American slang terms, found three such effects. First, Jin reproduced stereotypes of hyperheterosexual African American masculinity through his use of AAVE slang terms, such as "booty," which emphasizes the objectification of female bodies. Second, through his appropriation of African American maleness, Jin used AAVE to negotiate his Korean American male identity by challenging stereotypes of Asian American men as passive and sexless. Third, Jin appropriated AAVE slang terms, such as "whitey," to criticize European American domination. This last indexical effect creates an alliance between Asian Americans and African Americans based on shared discrimination as people of color.

Like Jin, Sokla (Cambodian American male) metapragmatically constructed an explicit alliance between African Americans and Asian Americans but, unlike Jin, Sokla argued that the alliance only worked with a certain kind of Asian American: the Other Asian. As explained earlier, Sokla often distinguished between what he called Asian Americans, such as Chinese, Japanese, and Korean Americans (like Jin), and what he called the Other Asian, post-1975 Southeast Asian refugees (like Sokla). Sokla identified as the Other Asian because he claimed he shared little with Asian Americans (and European Americans) because of their different political, class, and immigrant histories in the United States. Rather, Sokla saw the Other Asian in a similar position as African Americans because they both struggled socioeconomically and "against White power." In short, Sokla argued, "We don't identify with Asians, so we identify with Blacks." So whereas Jin as a Korean American was able to forge a third indexical link that allowed him to create an alliance with African Americans in certain contexts, Sokla excluded middle-class East Asian Americans, like Jin, because African Americans shared a political and socioeconomic history with the Other Asian, not with other Asian Americans.

Although explicitly identifying with African Americans, Sokla had an ambiguous linguistic identification with African Americans. Sokla claimed that if he was not speaking Khmer (Cambodian), he was speaking a "borrowed language," which to him was an AAVE-influenced American English variety. Le Page and Tabouret-Keller (1985), who asserted that our folk notions create imagined links between a single language and a single identity, claimed that "[m]any communities hold stereotypes based on the idea of strict correlation between monolingual language use and univocal identity" (p. 243). Sokla complicated this notion with his hybrid sense of identity as the Other Asian: Although being Cambodian may have correlated to speaking Khmer, his identification with African Americans may have correlated to speaking AAVE. Yet although Sokla embraced African American social and linguistic practices, he also distanced himself through his use of the word "borrow." Morgan (2001) argued that "[o]ne can be sustained within their group and represent that group, but they may have to borrow from other groups to embellish their notion of membership and coolness across groups" (p. 2). Morgan's (2001) point about borrowing while sustaining is illustrated by Sokla, who complexified relationships between language and identity by borrowing from African Americans both to identify with African Americans and to fashion his identity as the Other Asian.

Because Sokla racialized his borrowing of slang as African American speech yet affiliated with African Americans, he achieved triple indexical effects when he spoke slang. In the following three excerpts from the 1999 teen-created video *American Sroksrei*, Sokla says "na mean" as he plays a fictional character, Azeil, modeled largely on himself. Azeil is an independent spirit, who sees gangs as unnecessary and finds strength instead in hip hop and break dancing. In each excerpt, in which Sokla is speaking as the character Azeil, is a token of "na mean" or "nya" [nja] (the shortened version of "na mean"), which are the only three instances of this slang phrase in the entire 15-min video.

(3)

```
14   Sokla:   I came from the Asian ghetto, seventh street …
15            it's just, y'know, the same thing in Cambodia.
16            it's just run down, na mean?
```

(4)

```
17   Sokla:   it's like only a few people, the kids y'know,
18            just like y'know just wanna try to make it, go
19            to school in order they can get an education,
20            and there's the other kids, those who don't
21            want to do that, nya? they just want to get
22            the fast money, y'know, sell drugs, stole,
23            y'know, just hung out, did nothin'
```

(5)

```
24   Sokla:   he try to come on to me like he's somethin',
25            y'know, and y'know him and his crew, wha:t,
26            cause I'm just by myself you gonna try and
27            pick on me? na mean y'know like I'll s-
28            s- y'know I don't care to get rolled on, teach
29            these people somethin'
```

Sokla used "na mean" (lines 6, 27) and "nya" (line 21) when speaking of ghetto areas (line 14), drug dealers (line 22), thieves (line 22), laziness (line 23) and violence (lines 24–29). His use of African American slang directly indexes himself as urban, hip, cool, and tough, while indirectly indexing African Americans as associated with deviant behaviors. But in addition, a third indexical effect constructs an alliance between Sokla and African Americans because by using slang, which he racialized as belonging to African Americans, Sokla revealed aspects of his life that were affiliated with African American struggles in terms of class (Sokla lived in a poor neighborhood in South Philadelphia), education (Sokla used to be suspicious of the promises of education), and lifestyle (Sokla used to be in a gang). Choosing to bare this image in a video for public consumption, Sokla told me that he wanted to connect his life as a Southeast Asian refugee to that of many African Americans to educate wider audiences about the struggles of growing up as a young person of color in a poor urban area.

AUTHENTICATION OF THE SLANG SPEAKER

Whereas Van and Sokla explicitly racialized slang as belonging to African Americans for dual or triple indexical effects, there were some teens who did not "other" slang but authenticated themselves as speakers of African American slang. For both types of youth, slang emerged with local linguistic capital. Bourdieu (1991) argued that competence in the legitimate language functions as linguistic capital. Unlike in Bourdieu, however, the legitimate language, within the local setting of the video-making project, emerged as slang and not as a codified, institutionalized, and normalized dominant language—namely Standard English—in formal markets. But Bourdieu's concept of a legitimate language is adaptable to local linguistic markets as similar issues arise, such as the imposition of slang as the legitimate language, its unequal distribution, and the devaluation of other modes of expression (cf. Eckert, 2000; Woolard, 1985, on alternative markets).

Youth-Adult Divider

The adult program staff at the video-making project aimed to organize a learning space that respected, listened to, and valued the local knowledge of youth (cf.

Heath & McLaughlin, 1993). In many ways, the adults tried to avoid replicating a teacher-centered, school-like space and instead tried to organize cooperative learning, where small groups of teens interacted to collectively achieve instructional goals. The curriculum included what teens themselves identified as important, and youth were involved in several aspects of program development and decision-making processes. In the Asian Arts Initiative space, adults generally respected the multiple ways in which teens expressed themselves, including nonverbal activity, such as clothing and break dancing, as well as verbal activity, such as cursing and slang.

Despite—or perhaps enabled by—the overall accepting attitude toward slang, youth often used slang to mark divisions between youth and adult identities. In these cases, instead of racializing slang as belonging to African Americans, some teens authenticated identities as slang speakers through foregrounding the function of slang as a marker of urban youth subcultural affiliation in which the teens claimed participation. This is exemplified in the following interaction, which took place during a scriptwriting session for the 2001 video *Ba. Bay. Three.* The video focuses on the forbidden interethnic relationship between Moi, a Cambodian American teenage girl, and Hoa, a Vietnamese American teenage boy. During the scriptwriting session, the adult scriptwriting artist, Didi (Indian American female), encounters the slang word "aite" for the first time. Didi and the teen scriptwriters, Jill (Haitian Cuban American female), Enoy (Cambodian Chinese American female), Cindy (Chinese Burmese American female) and Rod (Laotian American male), are writing the dialogue for Hoa, who expresses to his friend (who turns out to be Moi's brother) that he likes Moi as she walks by. Didi's dialogue suggestion, "she's kind of cute," is rejected by the teens, who prefer that the character speak slang: "She look kinda aite." As Didi desperately tries to understand what the teens are saying, the teens do not facilitate her comprehension of slang.

(6)

```
30    Didi:    ok so he- so Hoa [says she's- she's kind of=
31    Jill:                     [<writing> still watching
32    Didi:    =cute? and then yeah still wa-
33    Enoy:    nobody (gonna) use the word cute, it like i-
34             i- she look kinda aite
35    Didi:    yeah but what word will you use
```

```
36    Enoy:     she look kinda aite
37    Jill:     <writing> she (.) look (.) kinda (.) aite
38              (.) I can't spell (?)
39    Cindy:    [hmm hmm
40    Enoy:     [hmm hmm
41    Jill:     that's all right (they're not gonna like this)
42    Rod:      <pointing to the word "look" that Jill wrote>
43              erase this
44    Jill:     <writing> still (walking)
45    Rod:      she's kinda aite
46    Didi:     she's [kinda what? (1.1) <leaning in and=
47    Jill:           [she look kinda aite
48    Didi:     =reading what Jill wrote> aite
49    Enoy:     [aite
50    Jill:     [aite
51    Didi:     oh [I ge(hh)t i(hh)t heh heh
52    Jill:        [heh heh
53    Cindy:       [heh heh
54    Jill:     <pointing to her left with thumb> they'll know
55              what we're talking about heh heh
```

In this interaction, slang emerges with local linguistic capital, as Didi is set in opposition to a shared youth identity. After Didi suggests that Hoa could say the word "cute" (lines 30, 32), Enoy explicitly rejects Didi's contribution—"nobody (gonna) use the word cute" (line 33)—then proposes that he should say "aite" instead (line 34), which is subsequently taken up by the other teens. While slang is established as the legitimate language as "aite" replaces "cute"—a mainstream American English word suggested by an adult—an in-group of teens against which Didi is positioned is constituted. Didi is further removed from this group of teens when she displays that she does not know the word "aite," and the teens do not facilitate her comprehension. Didi asks, "but what word will you use" (line 35), then has to ask again, "she's kinda what?" (line 46), as Enoy and Jill just simply repeat "aite" (lines 47, 49–50) when they could have enunciated "all right" to help Didi understand.[3]

Pronominal Indexicals

Accompanied by pronominal indexicals, such as "they" and "we," slang functions to further solidify a distinct boundary between the adult out-group and the youth in-group. In the sentence uttered by Jill, "they'll know what we're talking about" (lines 54–55), I argue that "we" indexes a group that includes only the teens in the immediate interaction, and not the adult, whereas "they" indexes a group that includes only the other teens, and no adults. Thus both "they" and "we" constitute two groups that consist of only teens, and adults are excluded from the indexical field.

First, although "they" has some indexical ambiguity, it becomes solidified as an index of a group that consists of only teens outside of the immediate interaction. This is because Jill accompanies the indexical "they" with a gesture that is partly decipherable with appeal to both cotext (what is said before and after) and context (aspects of the interaction). In terms of cotext, Jill says "they" earlier in the interaction in "they're not going to like this" (line 41) to refer to the other teens because they, not the adult staff, were in the highest position to evaluate the development of the script. In terms of context, because adult staff and other teen participants were outside of the room and in the direction in which Jill is pointing, it is possible that she is referring to both teens and adults with "they." However, if "they'll know what we're talking about," then "they" must also be a group of people who understands slang. Because Didi had so much trouble understanding "aite," she and perhaps the other adults are not in-

---

[3]Bucholtz (1997) similarly found that the non -African American students in her study did not facilitate their teachers' comprehension of AAVE or slang terms, whereas the African American students generally did. She argued that this is the case because African Americans, as racial minorities, are used to accommodating mainstream English speakers. Thus, the European American students were able to appropriate AAVE without appropriating the obligation to accommodate. The teens in this study complicated a Black-White racial paradigm because Asian Americans are minorities, too. Yet at least some of the teens in this study were more like Bucholtz's European American youth, considering that AAVE styles were constructed as "borrowed" by some teens, such as Van and Sokla. Moreover, in contrast to Bucholtz's school setting, the informality of the video-making project and of Didi's role as "artist" instead of "teacher" may have produced a lesser power differential, making the teens more comfortable not accommodating.

cluded in "they," further establishing adults as the out-group and teens as the in-group.

Moreover, I argue that Jill's use of exclusive "we" in "they'll know what we're talking about" serves to further constitute a teen in-group that is set apart from an adult out-group. Although "we" could potentially include everyone in the immediate interaction, it is more likely that "we" indexes only the teens because Didi's membership in an out-group was established through several indexical cues. Displays of incomprehension by Didi, while teens engage in the production, comprehension, writing, and negotiation of slang suggest that Didi is not included in Jill's "we." Rather, Jill's utterance serves to further distance Didi from the group of teens. Although both "they" and "we" assign teens to a group of authenticated users of slang, adults are constantly pushed into an out-group that lacks familiarity with youth slang, the interactionally emergent legitimate language.

Youth-Youth Divider

Not only could slang unify youth against adults like Didi, but it could also create divisions of identity among youth. Although many researchers note that slang can mark youth subcultural participation and resistance to power structures, few studies consider how slang can be used to divide youth identities. Yet the divisions among different groups of youth are often more relevant and meaningful to teenagers than the divisions between youth and adults (Bucholtz, in press). Thus, I turn to a discussion of the ways in which some teens interactionally positioned themselves in opposition to other teens based on authenticated identities as speakers of African American slang. In these interactions, slang competency was measured less by linguistic accuracy and more by other aspects of social identity that emerged through the interactional details of talk. That is, the teens who were authenticated and authenticated themselves as speakers of African American slang emerged with local authority and prestige based on a poor and working-class South Philadelphia identity with close ties to African Americans. These same teens positioned themselves as slang teachers and others as their students.

The following interaction, which took place during a project session in 2002, reveals the function of slang as a divider of youth identities. Anh (Vietnamese Cambodian Chinese American female), Will (Chinese American male),

Macy (Vietnamese American female), Chea (Cambodian Vietnamese Chinese American male), and Van (Vietnamese American female) are in a small group, working on the script for the 2002 video *These Are the Days*, which is about a teenage couple, JJ and Nara, who break up because of pressures from friends and from JJ's past with his ex-girlfriend, Ling. The following interaction begins with Anh and Will reading the parts of JJ's friends in the script. Will's perform-ance of "na mean" invites ridicule and coaching by other teens.

(7)

```
56   Anh:    <reading script> there's something about Ling
57           that Nara can't be
58   Will:   <reading script> she's missing something na
59           mean heh heh heh
60   Anh:    mm, na mean? na na
61   Will:   na
62   Anh:    na mean
63   Will:   na mean
64   Macy:   na mean [you gotta say that
65   Will:          [na mean
66   Will:   na [mean
67   Macy:      [na::::
68   Anh:    na mean
69   Will:   na:::: mean
70   Van:    ha ha ha ha you said na:::: mean
71   Macy:   <tapping Anh on her shoulder> do you know Jen?
72           do you know Jen Morgan?
73   Anh:    no
74   Macy:   she's so::: like- (0.8) her English is
75           perfect, (like) really perfect and you try to
76           teach her slang and stuff and it is so cute
77           (1.8) <smiles>
78   Anh:    <frowning> na mean it's like trying to teach
79           Miss Carter how to speak slang
```

An interactionally emergent division positions Anh, Macy, and Van in one group and Will in another group based on authoritative stances toward African American slang. After Will reads the line in the script (lines 58–59), Anh and then Macy start modeling "na mean" for Will and coaching him on how to say it. Macy points out the vowel elongation that Will needs to focus on, "na::::" (line 67). After Will tries to elongate the vowel, Van laughs and mocks Will's performance (line 70). Anh, Macy, and Van emerge as slang authorities, able to judge and ridicule Will's performance of slang. Anh and Macy, in particular, emerge as authenticated speakers of African American slang, trying to teach their student, Will, how to speak it.

Parallel Denotational Texts
With Conflicting Metapragmatic Commentary

Functioning to further solidify Will as African American slang incompetent, Macy and Anh introduce denotational texts that run parallel to the denotational and interactional texts at hand. Denotational text is the coherent representation of content in an interaction; in the interactional text, a recognizable interaction coheres as the interactants are positioned in socially meaningful ways (Silverstein, 1993). Before Macy and Anh begin discussing the teaching of slang to others (lines 71–79), the denotational text emerges as a slang lesson for Will, and the interactional text emerges with Will positioned as the student, Macy and Anh as his teachers, and Van as someone who is able to evaluate Will's progress. But when Macy and Anh begin discussing teaching slang to others—Jen Morgan and Miss Carter—in the middle of Will's lesson, the denotational text shifts from a slang lesson for Will to slang lessons for Jen Morgan and Miss Carter. Macy explains that her friend Jen Morgan's "English is perfect" (lines 74–75), and when Macy teaches her slang it is "so cute" (line 76). Because this story emerges in the middle of her slang lesson with Will, Macy may be drawing a parallel between Macy teaching Jen slang and Macy teaching Will slang. Through parallel textuality, Macy may be grouping Will with Jen as people who speak Standard English and are cute when they try to speak slang.

Anh offers another parallel denotational text but with a conflicting metapragmatic commentary. When Anh says, "it's like trying to teach Miss Carter how to speak slang" (lines 78–79), she frowns, which suggests that the act of teaching Miss Carter slang or that Miss Carter herself is unpleasant. Miss Carter, who is a teacher at their school, may not be "cute" like Jen. Also, Miss Carter, who is an adult like Didi and outside their social group, may present a hopeless situation where, no matter how hard they try to teach her slang, she simply cannot speak it. Though Anh, like Macy, produces a denotational parallel between Anh teaching Miss Carter slang and Anh teaching Will slang, she provides a metapragmatic commentary that contradicts Macy's. That is, instead of grouping Will with cute Jen, Anh may be grouping Will with hopeless Miss Carter.

Macy and Anh, thus, produce two different denotational texts, which accomplish two different interactional positions for Will. Although Anh and Macy are both teaching Will slang and both constructing and positioning Will as incompetent in slang, they draw different kinds of boundaries between youth identities. Macy's story of Jen Morgan interactionally positions Will as a Standard English speaker who is cute when he learns slang. Anh's story of Miss Carter interactionally positions Will as a hopeless outsider of Anh's social group of slang speakers. Thus, the effects of the stories of Jen Morgan and Miss Carter serve as conflicting metapragmatic commentary on the immediate interaction of Anh and Macy teaching Will slang.

Place as Implicit Index of Class and Race

After the two parallel denotational texts are introduced by Macy and Anh, Will draws attention back to himself as he softly attempts to produce African American slang again.

(8)

```
80   Will:    °na mean°
81   Anh:     all right say aite
82   Will:    aite (0.8)
83   Macy:    aite
84   Anh:     aite
85   Will:    aite
86   Macy:    you gotta say it with some pi[zzazz
87   Anh:                                  [<gazing at Chea>
88            na mean
89   Chea:    na mean (0.9)
90   Anh:     <smiling and extending and bouncing left hand
91            palm up toward Chea while gazing at Macy then
92            Will>
93   Macy:    good job Chea
94   Anh:     Chea's from South Philly of course
```

```
95   Will:    heh I'm from Northeast
96   Macy:    yeah
97   Will:    I'm from the suburb
98   Anh:     I know
99   Will:    I'm from the suburb
100  Macy:    us South people
101  Will:    I'm from the suburb man
```

As Anh and Macy continue to teach Will slang, they draw on ideologies that link slang to region, which authenticates them and Chea as speakers of African American slang. Considering the parallel denotational text of hopeless, out-grouped Miss Carter, Anh might be signaling her frustration with hopeless, out-grouped Will and his performance of "na mean" by moving on to "aite" (line 81). Just as they did with "na mean," Macy and Anh provide corrective feedback to Will through modeling and coaching. Then, Anh pulls Chea into the lesson as she asks him to model "na mean" for Will (lines 87–88). Chea complies and receives praise from Macy (line 93) and Anh, who extends her hand proudly toward Chea (lines 90–92). Then, the connection between slang and region is made denotationally explicit. Chea is regarded as an authenticated speaker of African American slang because he lives in "South Philly" (line 94), which is where Anh and Macy also live (line 100), whereas Will lives in the northeastern suburbs (lines 95, 97, 99, 101).

Although region is explicitly identified as the main marker dividing youth identities, socioeconomic status and proximity to African Americans are implicitly indexed as additional, if not more precise, social markers of an authenticated speaker of African American slang (cf. Sweetland, 2002). Anh, Macy, and Chea live in poor and working-class neighborhoods in South Philadelphia with large African American populations, whereas Will lives in a suburb in Northeast Philadelphia populated primarily by middle-class European Americans. Although class and race are not explicitly mentioned, they are the unmarked social factors that are implicitly linked to the salience of place in the authentication of a speaker of African American slang. After all, it is largely socioeconomic status that determines place of residence, rather than place of residence determining socioeconomic status. The intricate links between place, race, and class create the implicit formula that teens invoke to authenticate themselves or others as speakers of African American slang.

CONCLUSION

This chapter reveals the multiple ways in which Southeast Asian American teenagers invoked stereotypes linked to African American slang in the construction of their own identities. Whereas some of the teens racialized African American slang, others authenticated identities as slang speakers. The precarious position of Asian Americans—and particularly post-1975 Southeast Asian refugees—in U.S. ideologies of race allowed the teens to establish various identities in relation to urban youth culture and African American stereotypes. Because the Other Asian identity disrupts the binary positioning of Asian Americans as honorary Whites or forever foreigners, the problem minority stereotype of Southeast Asian refugees aligned some teens more closely with the location of African Americans in U.S. racial discourses. Van and Sokla's slang use relied on stereotypes of African Americans to construct their own identities as tough, threatening, and violent. Drawing on these stereotypes simultaneously aligned Van and Sokla with the problem minority stereotype of Asian Americans. Thus, I argue that rather than trying to "act Black," the teens used African American stereotypes as resources to fashion their own identities as the Other Asian.

Teens also used slang to signal urban youth subcultural participation by constructing divisions of identity between youth and adults and between each other. Rather than explicitly racializing "na mean" and "aite" as African American slang terms as Van and Sokla did, other teens authenticated themselves as slang speakers based on an explicit indexical link they created between slang and residence, namely South Philadelphia. Though region emerged with discursive salience, I argue that it implicitly indexed other aspects of identity—including proximity to African Americans—as markers of an authenticated slang speaker. Although accomplished more implicitly than Van and Sokla, Anh and Macy nonetheless proved that drawing on African American stereotypes was once again critical in constructing their own Asian American urban youth identities.

By closely examining both metapragmatic discussions of slang and the emergence of slang in interaction, this chapter reveals the various ways in which the teenagers both talked about and used slang in the making of youth identity. Traditional approaches to slang research that rely on quantitative measures to elicit definitions and ideologies of slang fail to capture how identities are constituted through often subtle and intricate discursive practices, such as dual, triple, and pronominal indexicality, parallel denotational texts, and implicit metapragmatic commentary. Although racialization and authentication emerged as two possible orientations toward slang that allowed the Asian American teens to creatively establish affiliations with African Americans and participation in urban youth subcultural styles, slang research—as it continues to take a linguistic anthropological and discourse approach—will be able to discover more ways in which slang is used in the articulation of youth identities. The next chapter also takes a discourse approach to questions of stereotype and identity, but instead of examining how the teens used African American stereotypes to construct their identities in relation to other racial groups, I explore how the teens used Asian American stereotypes to construct panethnicity among Asian American ethnic groups.

4

From Storeowners to Minivan Drivers: Building Panethnicity With Asian American Stereotypes

Asian people ... they always got to own something.

—Dan, 2001

Perhaps not surprisingly, the topic of Asian American panethnicity was frequently discussed at the after-school teen video-making project and at the Asian Arts Initiative, where the project took place. In conversations about the organizational philosophy and mission, staff members often emphasized how the Asian Arts Initiative was a community arts alliance that targeted and engaged diverse Asian American ethnic groups in its outreach and programming. On the whole, adult and youth voices were consistent and united with respect to the goal of fostering a sense of panethnic Asian American community in the Philadelphia area. The teens were, after all, voluntarily participating in a panethnic Asian American community arts organization. Most of the teens also belonged to panethnic Asian American friendship groups, which they formed either prior to or during their time at the video-making project.

Among the more politically engaged teens, such as Sokla (Cambodian American male), panethnicity was understood as a socially constructed device for unifying diverse peoples for a common purpose, whether for video making, for protesting, or for reaching other mutual goals. Despite the profound differences between ethnic groups, Sokla claimed that identifying with monolithic communities of race and class brought more numbers behind a unified voice and aided in political mobilization around issues of racism and socioeconomic injustice. For example, Sokla, several other teens, staff members, and I united with the Asian American community in Philadelphia to collectively protest against the building of a stadium in Chinatown in 2000. Coming together as a panethnic community momentarily suppressed issues of difference between and within Asian American ethnic groups for the benefit of social activism.

Throughout the years, however, Sokla's views on panethnic Asian American community often clashed with those of the Asian Arts Initiative staff, particularly during one of his conversations in 2000 with two staff members: Olive (Japanese American female) and Mark (Filipino American male). On this day, Olive was questioning Sokla about why he did not identify as Asian American, a label that Olive tended to embrace. This conversation was reminiscent of the one Sokla had a year earlier (see chapter 1), and he proceeded to tell Olive his usual reasons: He was Asian, not Asian American, because he was not born in the United States; he felt historically, politically, and socioeconomically separate from Chinese and Japanese Americans, whom he saw as Asian Americans; as a post-1975 Southeast Asian refugee—the Other Asian—he did not feel that his interests were addressed by the Asian American movement. Mark walked by during Sokla and Olive's conversation and said that he agreed with Olive about the importance of identifying as Asian American. Mark continued to challenge Sokla by asking him why he was at the Asian Arts Initiative if he did not identify with the Asian American community. In a play on words, Sokla claimed, "Because it's the Asian Arts Initiative, not the Asian *American* Arts Initiative."

Rather than interpreting the mercurial nature of Sokla's self-identification as an identity crisis, I see it as indicative of the importance of conversational context. In certain interactions, particularly when political activism was foregrounded, Sokla identified as Asian American. When Sokla refused to identify as Asian American, he was interacting with people from different backgrounds who identified as Asian American: For example, whereas Sokla was Cambodian American, Olive and Mark were Japanese American and Filipino American, respectively; whereas Sokla was foreign born, Olive and Mark were American born; whereas Sokla's family was poor, Olive and Mark were middle class. Perhaps more important, Sokla's opposition was likely guided by other interactional factors, such as Olive's and Mark's persistent attempts to limit Sokla's identity options by insisting he identify as Asian American. Sokla resisted being restricted to this identity label, a label with which both Olive and Mark identified. Complying would not only force Sokla into a group identity that he was uncomfortable with for various social and economic reasons, but it would also locate

Sokla as a member of the same group as Olive and Mark, people who did not necessarily relate to his experience as the Other Asian.

Similar to the context-dependent ways in which Sokla played with racial categories and ethnic distinctions to argue for or against panethnicity, these next two chapters examine conversational contexts in which panethnicity was locally produced or dismantled among the Asian American teenagers at the video-making project. Because notions of race, ethnicity, and panethnicity are explored as macrolevel concepts in much of the research literature, these chapters explore the flexibility of these categories in local discursive practice. In this chapter, I examine how conversations about stereotypes momentarily redrew racial and ethnic community boundaries as ethnic-specific stereotypes were widened and applied to a larger panethnic Asian American community in which the teens claimed membership. Asian American stereotypes—which link behaviors to groups within certain racial and ethnic scopes—are prime sites for witnessing such ethnic boundary making. Although stereotypes are often perceived as negative, homogenizing representations used to oppress people, the teens demonstrated how stereotypes can be reappropriated for creative purposes, such as constructing identities, building social relationships, achieving community solidarity, and producing panethnicity.

RACE, ETHNICITY, AND PANETHNICITY AS INTERACTIONAL CONSTRUCTS

Although there is no scientific evidence to support their biological importance, race and ethnicity are still commonly perceived as primordial and natural categories. Subscribing to human divisions based on concepts of race and ethnicity, people—not biology or nature—uphold this social order (Le Page & Tabouret-Keller, 1985). Several scholars thus argue that race and ethnicity are socially constructed concepts. As powerful categories that organize social life, race and ethnicity play a major role in how people are defined and define themselves, particularly in the United States. The concepts of race and ethnicity achieve extraordinary social importance because they are deeply rooted in the institutional structures of many societies, profoundly affecting the everyday lives of individuals.

According to Waters (1990), "race" refers to distinctions drawn from physical appearance, and "ethnicity" refers to distinctions based on national origin, language, religion, food, and other cultural markers. Omi and Winant (1994) similarly argued that people construct race in reference to different human body types. Although both Waters and Omi and Winant recognized that race and ethnicity are social and political constructs, their mutual emphasis on perceptions of race as based on phenotype has been called into question. Bailey (2002), for example, revealed how Dominican Americans construct racial identities not on the basis of phenotype but on the basis of language. Though others may perceive them in racial terms (e.g., "Black"), Dominican Americans construct their identities along ethnolinguistic lines (e.g., "Spanish"). The idea of phenotype-based racial categorization falls further apart when applied to ethnic groups, such as Cambodian and Japanese, who are perceived as part of the same race (i.e., "Asian"), though they share little in common in terms of physical appearance. Shared phenotype not only fails to define racial groups, but it also fails to define ethnic groups. Filipinos, for example, exhibit diverse physical bodies due to the blending of various racial and ethnic groups caused by the complex colonial, immigrant, and socioeconomic histories in the Philippines. Such mixing across national and cultural borders in an ever-increasing globalized economy makes efforts to define race and ethnicity by their content ultimately fail, revealing instead how slippery and elusive these categories are.

Hence several scholars are interested not in the content of ethnic groups but in the construction of ethnic boundaries. Barth (1969), who formulated ethnicity as a function of boundary maintenance, was concerned not with the internal inventories of groups but with how groups create borders between them. Such practices are vividly revealed at the level of interaction. Linguistic anthropologists and discourse analysts, in particular, closely examine the complex ways in which boundaries between ethnic groups are locally constituted, revealing how ethnic identity is not a fixed property of individuals but a social achievement produced through interaction. Rampton (1995a), for example, examined how ethnically diverse adolescent peer groups problematize the formation and maintenance of ethnicity. He argued that youth transgress ethnic boundaries by crossing into languages associated with other ethnic groups, creating new ethnicities (Hall, 1988), ethnicities produced through emergent communities in contact and thus predicated on difference and diversity, not on primordial bonds. Other studies revealed how different ethnic identities become established within what seems to be a single ethnic group: For example, Mendoza-Denton (1996) showed how Mexican American gang girls identify as either "Sureñas" (linked to Spanish-dominant first generation) or "Norteñas" (linked to English-dominant second generation), and Kang (2004) revealed how Korean American camp counselors constituted themselves as either "Korean" (linked to teaching cultural heritage) or "Korean American" (linked to being a mentor). Studies such as these reveal how ethnicity cannot be defined by what it consists of; rather, ethnic identities are creatively produced in relation to ideological divisions constituted in discursive practice.

Because larger social forces also influence the types of identities available to individuals, the question of how people linguistically navigate racial and ethnic categories is incomplete without considering the institutions within which these interactions occur. The conversations I analyze in this chapter occurred among Asian American teenagers who were participating in a video-making project at an organization that promoted Asian American panethnicity. Panethnicity, which is the merging of groups of different national origins into new larger scale groupings (Nagel, 1982; Padilla, 1985), has been used as a tool to unite various ethnic groups to protect and promote collective interests (Espiritu, 1992). Asian American panethnicity emerged during the civil rights movement in the 1960s to mobilize diverse Asian American ethnic groups for a common political cause. In a similar spirit, the Asian Arts Initiative saw itself as a catalyst for social change and thus valued panethnicity as it brought together the ethnically diverse Asian American teens to engage in the collective production of a video. Because Asian Americans constitute a heterogeneous group, panethnicity is not unproblematic because it sometimes leads people, like Sokla, to feel that their interests are not being met because other ethnic groups are the driving force behind large-scale panethnic movements. Yet panethnicity, I argue, does not operate exclusively along broad dimensions; it can also be a precisely local and flexible production in interactions. In the conversations about stereotypes that follow, the very elasticity of ethnic and racial boundaries allowed the Asian American teens in this study to readjust ethnic borders and transgress ethnic lines in the making of Asian American panethnicity.

ASIAN MARTIAL ARTS EXPERT STEREOTYPE

Among the many Asian American stereotypes that affected the daily lives of the teenagers was the Asian martial arts expert stereotype. Several teens resented this stereotype, claiming that it was common for non-Asians in their schools and neighborhoods to assume that they knew martial arts. Other teens, however, gleaned some value from it. Chea (Cambodian Vietnamese Chinese American male), for example, explained to me that his high school classmates "always think Asian guys some kind of fobbish[1] super fighting guy." He reported that his peers verbally assaulted him with phrases like "won ton soup" or "ching-chong-chang," while ordering him to perform martial arts moves. Yet Chea thought that the Asian martial arts expert stereotype also protected him in some ways: Because his peers assumed that he knew martial arts, they were afraid to physically attack him. Unlike the F.O.B. stereotype, which Chea perceived as always negative, the Asian martial arts stereotype achieved some practical value in his life.

Not only did others apply the Asian martial arts expert stereotype to the teens, but the teens also applied the stereotype to themselves. This section analyzes one such interaction in which the Asian American teens invoked the Asian martial arts stereotype. The interaction occurred at a video-making project session in 2002, where the participants were divided into small groups. Each group had to write and shoot a short scene about gender and sexism, which could potentially go into the final script of the 2002 video *These Are the Days*. The following interaction occurred among one small group. The main interactants are two teens: Will (Chinese American male) and Van (Vietnamese American female). There are also two other teens, Jerry (Chinese American male) and Chea, and three adults, Derek (Filipino American male), Edie (Chinese American female), and Lily (Chinese American female). The teens in this group decided to write a scene with a husband and wife. In the scene, the husband is angry because the wife refuses to get a job, and the wife is angry because the husband does not help with the housework. After Will suggests that Van be the wife, the others designate Will as the husband. The following excerpt begins as Will is trying to get out of the husband role.

---

[1]"Fobbish" is derived from "F.O.B." (Fresh Off the Boat), a derogatory label for recently arrived Asian immigrants. See chapter 2 for an extended discussion of how the term F.O.B. was used and understood by the teens.

(1)

```
1    Van:     if you quit the girls in this group are taking
2             you down <bouncing right index finger down and
3             in front of her>
4    Will:    what, by all of you? heh heh <moving right
5             hand left to right in front of Jerry, Van and
6             Chea, slaps knee once>
7    Van:     we're gonna do some Crouching Tiger, Hidden
8             Dragon on you:: <bouncing right index finger
9             down>
10   Chea:    hh hh <smiling>
11   Lily:    ha ha ha ha ha
12   Van:     heh heh <looking at Lily>
```

Crouching Tiger, Hidden Dragon (A. Lee, 2002), a Chinese language martial arts film that achieved remarkable mainstream success in the United States, is used as an interactional resource by Van. Van makes the martial arts stereotype relevant by invoking the title of the film (lines 7–8), which adds emphasis to her playful threat to Will that the "girls in this group are taking you down" (lines 1–2). *Crouching Tiger, Hidden Dragon*, which boasts two central characters that are strong and powerful women, enables Van to construct a distinctly gendered identity as she highlights the fact that the girls will be the ones to harm Will. Will, who is upset at all of the interactants for pressuring him to play the husband role, shrugs off her threat and attempts to insult the male teens, Jerry and Chea, by using a hand gesture to indicate that Jerry, Van, and Chea are the girls in their group (lines 4–6). Even though many teens at the video-making project claimed that they resented the martial arts stereotype, here they laugh at it (lines 10–12), perhaps signaling that it is permissible for Asian Americans to stereotype themselves. Stereotyping the self, thus, becomes a resource for Van in several ways. First, invoking *Crouching Tiger, Hidden Dragon* builds on her previous threat, which helps construct Van as a forceful female type. In addition, her clever phrasing, "Crouching Tiger, Hidden Dragon on you" (lines 7–8), provokes laughter from others in the interaction, which serves to reflect positively on Van. Finally, invoking the stereotype helps Van command an audience and recruit them to achieve her local interactional goal of making Will play the husband. In the end, Van triumphed in committing Will to the role.

By invoking *Crouching Tiger, Hidden Dragon,* Van temporarily redrew ethnic boundaries by applying an ethnic-specific Chinese martial arts expert stereotype to herself, a Vietnamese American. By reappropriating this stereotype, it is possible that Van was traversing ethnic borders within a racial field, allowing herself, as Asian American, to inhabit a Chinese stereotype. However, it seems more likely that Van was not so much transgressing ethnic lines as she was reconfiguring ethnic scopes. That is, Van may have broadened the scope of the ethnic-specific Chinese martial arts stereotype, transforming it into a wider Asian American stereotype that could be more easily applied to herself. This practice of stereotype extension is not limited to Van alone; it is also encountered in the local neighborhoods of the teens as well as in wider societal discourses that circulate the Asian martial arts expert stereotype. By recontextualizing a stereotype as broadly Asian American and as maximally applicable to herself, Van locally produced an Asian American panethnicity to which she willingly claimed membership.

ASIAN FOOD STEREOTYPES

After Will eventually succumbed to the group pressure to play the role, Will and Van started to role-play the scene between husband and wife. Improvising, the two entered and maintained a performance frame in which they enacted a married couple: Will as breadwinner and Van as domestic keeper. During their role play, although Van as wife acknowledged that Will as husband bought the food, she focused on what she saw as the more important role: preparing the food. After Van established this, the two of them began invoking food items and arguing over who was the more competent cook. The following interaction begins after Van emphasized Will's inability to cook food.

(2)

```
13    Will:    I can cook, want to see me cook some rice?
14             <pulling right hand up left arm to his sleeve>
15    Van:     I can cook rice too <leaning in toward Will,
16             pointing to her chest with left index finger,
17             wobbling head side to side with chin out>
18    Will:    (cook) chicken?
```

```
19   Van:    I cook better rice heh heh
20   Will:   I cook better rice <slaps knee>
21   Van:    I cook better rice <slaps knee>
22   Will:   I do <leaning in toward Van>
23   Van:    I do
24   Will:   I do <leaning closer to Van>
25   Van:    I do
26   Will:   I do <leaning closer to Van>
```

Of all the food items to invoke, Will chooses the quintessential stereotype of Asian food: rice (line 13). Rice is a culinary staple in several Asian diets, including Chinese, which is Will's ethnic background, and Vietnamese, which is Van's. Even though Will and Van are members of different ethnic groups, Will invokes rice, which they can relate to as members of the same racial group. Although they escalate their playful opposition against each other, the invocation of rice places both Will and Van in a community of shared cultural reference based on an Asian American panethnic grouping. Rice is presupposed as a typical food cooked in their imagined home. Thus, Will invokes rice not only as a culturally appropriate resource for defying his wife but also to set the stage for a particular panethnic Asian American cultural production in which their imagined family maintains and produces an Asian culinary tradition in the United States.

As the interaction continues, both Van and Will invoke other food items, but this time in Vietnamese.

(3)

```
27   Van:    oh yeah? can you make pho?
28                              {beef noodle soup}
29   Will:   yeah I could make pho
30   Van:    (?) <closes eyes tightly, shakes head quickly>
31           s(hh)o can I:: hh
32   Will:   can you make cha gio
33                        {fried spring roll}
34   Van:    cha gio huh?
35   Will:   huh
36   Van:    yeah
37   Will:   yeah
38   Van:    yeah
```

```
39  Will:   yeah
40  Van:    yeah
41  Will:   yeah
42  Van:    can you make chao?
43                     {rice porridge}
44  Will:   yeah
45  Lily:   ha ha ha ha ha
46  Van:    yeah s(hh)o can I heh heh
47  Derek:  all right so you guys make a good married
48          [couple
49  Lily:   [yeah I know
50  Will:   no
51  Derek:  ha ha
```

Given their persistent efforts to outdo one another, it is clever of Van to ask Will if he can make pho, a Vietnamese soup (line 27). Unlike Will, who invokes rice, a food that both he and Van can equally relate to as Asian Americans, Van invokes pho, a food that is specific to Vietnamese and thus more closely linked to Van's ethnic background. This is not to assume, however, that because Will was Chinese American, he was unfamiliar with Vietnamese foods; in fact, most of the teens at the video-making project belonged to panethnic Asian American friendship groups and ate panethnic Asian foods. Lena (Chinese Cambodian Vietnamese American female), for example, claimed that even though she was ethnically Chinese, she knew many food names in Cambodian and Vietnamese. Yet invoking pho after invoking rice functions to reconfigure the categories of persona that are emerging through discourse. That is, the invocation of pho restricts the broad scope of rice-eating Asian Americans to a narrower group that privileges those most familiar with Vietnamese foods. Within this configuration Van, as Vietnamese American, is favored to emerge with more authority.

Yet Will claims he can make pho (line 29). He provides evidence for not only his familiarity with Vietnamese foods but also his Vietnamese linguistic ability by repeating the word pho. Although invoking pho had the potential to alienate Will because of his Chinese ethnic background, Will continues to fully engage in the interaction as he follows Van's lead by introducing another Vietnamese dish, Vietnamese spring rolls: "chao gio" (line 32). Thus, the ethnic boundaries that could have been narrowed to exclusively privilege Van actually open up. That is, by claiming Vietnamese foods as culturally familiar to him, Will redraws the ethnic boundaries in such a way that pho is not exclusively linked to Vietnamese but can also be claimed by other Asian Americans. This boundary reconfiguration continues to take shape as Van asks Will if he can make rice porridge in Vietnamese: "chao" (line 42). By invoking chao, Van could be doing numerous things: On the one hand, she could be testing Will's Vietnamese by introducing a lesser known Vietnamese dish; on the other hand, she could be presupposing that Will knows what chao is as she continues the cooking debate. In either case and regardless of Van's intentions, Asian American panethnicity further coheres as Will continues to claim Vietnamese foods as familiar to him, while his knowledge of the Vietnamese language and of Vietnamese dishes is left unchallenged. Thus, an Asian American panethnicity that forms unity among members of different ethnic groups, including Van and Will, is accomplished and foregrounded through the reappropriation of stereotypes of Asian and Vietnamese foods.

ASIAN STOREOWNER STEREOTYPE

Like the Asian martial arts expert stereotype, the Asian storeowner stereotype circulates widely in mass media. This stereotype operates within the model minority myth because it depicts Asian Americans as successful—yet often greedy and cheap (Sethi, 1994)—small business owners. Since the Los Angeles Riots in 1992, Asian American storeowners have come to precisely symbolize how minority groups are pitted against each other as one effect of the model minority stereotype (Prashad, 2002). Many argue that Korean-owned stores became the target of aggression because Asian Americans—as honorary Whites—were perceived as similar to the dominant majority and thus also to blame for the social and economic injustices against African Americans. Like the Asian martial arts expert stereotype, the Asian storeowner stereotype evoked diverse opinions among the teens: Some thought it was true; some thought it was oppressive; some thought it was funny. By analyzing how the Asian storeowner stereotype emerged in interactions, however, I discovered that these positions could be momentary and changeable depending on conversational context.

Similar to the ways in which Van and Will redrew the ethnic scopes of stereotypes, this section analyzes interactions in which the teens reconfigured the Asian storeowner stereotype in the production of Asian American panethnicity. The following interactions reveal how panethnicity is achieved in conjunction with other social actions, namely, positioning the self and other relative to stereotypes, constructing stereotyping as an oppressive practice to resist or as a panethnic resource to celebrate, and bringing about interactional effects from widely circulating stereotypes (e.g., Asian storeowner) that are different from those from locally circulating typifications (e.g., Asian minivan driver), what I call widespread typifications and local typifications, respectively. I show how the construction of panethnicity relies on the interrelationships among these social actions in two interactions in which the Asian storeowner stereotype is invoked.

A Brainstorming Activity

The first interaction I present occurred during a video-making project session in 2001. This session occurred early in the project year and was used to help explore possible themes for the video. Teens and adult artists and volunteers were divided into four small groups. Each small group had a private area and was given a large piece of paper on which to draw a large head in the center. After drawing the head, each group had to choose from a list of 5 statements and then write everything they could think of regarding that statement. The following interaction is from one of the small groups, which consisted of three teens: Moeun and Dan (Cambodian Chinese American males) and Anh (Vietnamese Cambodian Chinese American female). They were joined by two adults: Didi (Indian American female), who was the scriptwriting artist, and Kelly (Vietnamese American female), who was a project volunteer. All five were sitting in a circle around the piece of paper. They chose the statement "I feel different." When Anh was about to write on the inside of the head "mean," which teens claimed was something that their siblings thought of them, Didi stopped her and said, "No, this [pointing to the inside of the head] is what you really are, and this [pointing to the outside of the head] is what people think." Didi's directions made the activity particularly conducive to eliciting stereotypes because it involved an explicit distinction between what others thought of the teens and what the teens thought of themselves.

The following interaction begins with Moeun, who offers a suggestion for something to write on the outside of the head.

(4)

```
52   Moeun:   oh (.) put owns a Chinese restaurant
53   Anh:     <turns lips down, wrinkles forehead downward>
54   Didi:    o::h ok[ay(.) yeah that's a good idea heh heh
55   Moeun:         [heh heh
56   Anh:     owns a store? <picks up marker>
57   Moeun:   yeah
58   Didi:    yeah
59   Anh:     I own a s- my parents own a store <leans in to
60            write on paper, lips still turned down and
61            forehead wrinkled downward>
62   Moeun:   cause- Asian peop- cause like [Asian people=
63   Kelly:                                 [stereotypes
64   Moeun:   =yea:::h
65   Dan:     they always got to own something
66   Moeun:   yea::h
67   Kelly:   grocery store heh heh
68   Anh:     yeah I own a grocery store <turns lips down,
69            wrinkles forehead downward>
70   Moeun:   my parents too heh heh
71   Anh:     <turns lips up>
72   Dan:     drives minivan
73   Moeun:   heh heh
74   Anh:     o:h [yeah heh <gazes at Moeun, points to Dan>
75   Moeun:       [hell yeah hell [yeah if you don't drive=
76   Didi:                       [heh heh
77   Moeun:   =one you ain't Asian <gazes at Anh, points to
78            Dan> (1.9) drives minivan (4.6) heh heh
79   Anh:     my brother drives (psycho) people to work
80            every mo(hh)rning
81   Moeun:   heh heh
```

About a minute later, Olive (Japanese American female), another project volunteer, came into the room. She was curious about why they had "minivan" written down. "That's a stereotype?" she asked. Moeun replied, "That's what people think," and Anh clarified, "They think we drive minivans." Anh then paused and in a contemplative voice uttered, "But we do." Dan replied, "They shouldn't think that though."

A Scriptwriting Activity

The next interaction occurred at a scriptwriting session about 1 month later. The teen scriptwriters were Sara (Chinese American female), Enoy (Cambodian Chinese American female), Jill (Haitian Cuban American female), Rod (Laotian American male), and Cindy (Burmese Chinese American female). They were joined by the scriptwriting artist, Didi (Indian American female), who appeared in the previous interaction. In the following conversation, they are writing the first scene of the script for the 2001 video *Ba. Bay. Three.*, which focuses on the forbidden interethnic relationship between Moi, a Cambodian American teenage girl, and a Vietnamese American teenage boy. Yet during the time of the following interaction, the character of Moi was Chinese American, which the scriptwriters later changed to Cambodian American because they claimed that Cambodian-Vietnamese tensions were greater than Chinese-Cambodian tensions. In the following interaction, the scriptwriters are discussing what Moi's brother, Victor, is going to say to Moi in the first scene, which takes place on a basketball court after school. They want Victor to call Moi over to him, so the scriptwriters are thinking of reasons why he would need to do that.

The activity of scriptwriting, like the activity described in the previous section, can also be conducive to invoking stereotypes. Storytelling conventions and prior media representations of Asian Americans can function to restrict possibilities when developing characters in a script. As Didi, an experienced filmmaker, said about scriptwriting, "The first lines that come to your mind are usually stereotypes." The following interaction was no exception to her observation, but it was unlike the previous interaction in at least two ways. First, this scriptwriting activity was not asking for explicit distinctions between what others thought about the teens and what the teens thought about themselves. There was no specific discussion of whether the proposed reason for the boy calling his sister should or should not be a stereotypical idea about Asians. Second, as opposed to the previous activity in which what the teens discussed was mainly for their own benefit, the writing of a script for a video that was going to be viewed by audiences might have influenced the kind of material that participants would want to include. Although the teens might not have been wholly attuned to the potential consequences of their representations, the Asian Arts Initiative as a community organization was particularly sensitive to issues of representation. Thus, the potential reproduction of stereotypes was carefully monitored.

Before the following interaction began, Didi had asked the scriptwriters to come up with a line for Victor to say to his sister, Moi. Jill offers a suggestion.

(5)

```
82   Jill:   like mom [needs you at the- the store or=
83   Didi:            [I
84   Jill:   =something (0.8)
85   Didi:   mom needs you at the store? or (0.7)
86   Enoy:   I don't know (?)
87   Jill:   a lot of Chinese people do own a restaurant
88   Sara:   no they're not [owning a restaurant they're=₁
89   Enoy:                  [all right mom needs you to=₂
90   Sara:   ₁=not owning a restaurant
91   Enoy:   ₂=watch- mom needs you to watch the store.
92           they got to own something in their [life tell=
93   Sara:                                       [no no
94   Enoy:   =me your parents don't own anything in their
95           life <waving pencil with quick downward
96           motions in front of Sara's face>
97   Sara:   (?) in their life? they don't own anything
98           now, they did [but-
99   Enoy:                 [see see there you go <waving
100          pencil at Sara again, turns lips up, gazes at
101          Jill>
102  Sara:   but that's so:- [that's so stereotypical you=
103  Jill:                   [it's what.
104  Sara:   =cannot do that no [way no <slaps pencil=₁
105  Enoy:                      [heh heh yep all right=₂
106  Sara:   ₁=down, puts hands under table>
107  Enoy:   ₂=<puts hands under table, then brings them
108          back up> tell me tell me- um
109  Sara:   no: <puts hands palms facing out toward Enoy>
110  Enoy:   [they always- always no matter they got to=
111  Didi:   [what we have to do is-
112  Enoy:   =own some kind of store
113  Jill:   I know <counting on fingers> nail salon,
114          res[taurant, (???), hair salon
115  Enoy:      [<gazing at Jill, counting on fingers> hair
116          salon always (.) there's no joke- Manhattan
117          bagel (.) my uncle got a bagel store what the
```

```
118                hell is that? heh heh
119   Rod:         [heh heh
120   Jill:        [heh heh
121   Sara:        that's new that's new
122   Didi:        ok look it's really important-
123   Enoy:        they comin' up man <turns lips up, raises hand
124                palm up in front of Sara>
125   Sara:        <places head face down on table>
126   Didi:        u::h
127   Rod:         Asian bagel store ha ha
```

Identifying Stereotypes

Applying Putnam's (1975) description of a stereotype as typical features of a kind, this section identifies three linguistic elements in the two preceding transcripts to determine if stereotypes emerged in both interactions. The first element addresses what is "typical" by examining certain discursive features that index typicality, for example, adverbs such as "always." The second two elements address what is a "feature" and what is a "kind" by analyzing reference (kind) and predication (feature) (Wortham & Locher, 1996). Reference and predication function to relate some aspect of behavior (predication/feature) to a particular social category of persons (reference/kind). In the following excerpts taken from the earlier interactions, I use a triadic model to identify instances in which reference, predication, and what I call typicality devices together form stereotypes from the participant perspective.

(6) Reference: "Chinese people"; predication: "do own a restaurant"; typicality device: "a lot of" (plural quantifier)

```
87    Jill:     a lot of Chinese people do own a restaurant
```

(7) Reference: "Asian people" anaphorically indexed by "they"; predication: "own something"; typicality devices: "always" (adverb), "got to" (aspect marker)

```
62    Moeun:    cause- Asian peop- cause like [Asian people=
63    Kelly:                                  [stereotypes
64    Moeun:    =yea:::h
```

```
65   Dan:     they always got to own something
66   Moeun:   yea::h
```

(8) Reference: "Chinese people" (line 87) anaphorically indexed by "they"; predication: "own some kind of store"; typicality devices: "always" (adverb), "no matter" (phrasal adverb), "got to" (aspect marker)

```
110  Enoy:    [they always- always no matter they got to=
111  Didi:    [what we have to do is-
112  Enoy:    =own some kind of store
```

(9) Reference: "Asian people" (line 62) anaphorically indexed by "you"; predications: "don't drive one" ("minivan" line 72), "ain't Asian"; typicality device: "if you don't ... you ain't" (conditional embedded clause)

```
75   Moeun:      [hell yeah hell [yeah if you don't drive=
76   Didi:                       [heh heh
77   Moeun:   =one you ain't Asian <gazes at Anh, points to
```

In Examples 6–8, the Asian storeowner is recognized as a stereotype from the perspective of participants in both interactions. But whether it is a stereotype relies on knowledge of its circulation beyond these two interactions. Because U.S. news and entertainment media distribute the image of the Asian storeowner on a national scale, it is safe to say that the Asian storeowner is indeed a stereotype, or what I call a widespread typification, because of its societal circulation. In Example 9, on the other hand, teens from the first interaction seem to formulate what they interpret as a stereotype, that of the "Asian minivan driver." Yet because the image of the Asian minivan driver has a limited scope—as narrow as this particular interaction and as wide as perhaps Asian American communities in the Philadelphia area—I do not define it as a stereotype but as a local typification.

Participants also identified the Asian storeowner as a stereotype by explicitly calling it a stereotype. Such instances are known as denotationally explicit metapragmatic signs (Silverstein, 1993), which, when coupled with subsequent uptake or agreement by others, constitute another way to recognize how participants identify stereotypes.

(10) Denotationally explicit metapragmatic sign: "stereotypes"; uptake: "yea:::h"

```
62   Moeun:   cause- Asian peop- cause like [Asian people=
63   Kelly:                                 [stereotypes
64   Moeun:   =yea:::h
```

(11) Denotationally explicit metapragmatic sign: "stereotypical"; uptake: "heh heh yep"

```
102   Sara:   but that's so:- [that's so stereotypical you=
103   Jill:                   [it's what.
104   Sara:   =cannot do that no [way no <slaps pencil=₁
105   Enoy:                      [heh heh yep all right=₂
```

With the Asian storeowner identified as a stereotype that emerged in both inter-actions, the next three sections examine how the teens positioned themselves and others relative to stereotypes, constructed stereotyping as an oppressive practice or a panethnic resource, and brought about different effects from wide-spread typifications than from local typifications.

Positioning the Self and Other Relative to Stereotypes

One thing that the teens did with the Asian storeowner stereotype was use it as a resource for positioning themselves and each other as certain types of people. There were two kinds of positioning at issue here: teens positioning themselves with respect to the stereotype and teens positioning themselves with respect to each other. The first issue is concerned with the relationship between the deno-tational text and the interactional text (Silverstein, 1993), that is, with how the events discussed in the denotational text (i.e., stereotypes) relate to the partici-pants in the interactional text (i.e., the teens). With the exception of Jill (Haitian Cuban American female), that the Asian American teens invoked an Asian American stereotype foregrounded the potential for inhabiting the stereotype be-cause the teens saw themselves as Asian and some of the teens' families owned stores. Interactional positioning (Gergen & Kaye, 1992; Wortham, 2001), which is primarily concerned with how the interactants are positioning themselves with respect to each other in the interactional text, can be operationalized to explore the second issue of how the teens constructed identities and relationships with one another.

In the following excerpts, both Anh and Sara are the first to position themselves as inhabiting the Asian storeowner stereotype by admitting that their families own or have owned stores. To inhabit a stereotype, I argue that one must locate oneself or be located as a member of both the reference (in this case, "Asian") and the predication (in this case, "owns store"). As Anh and Sara inhabit this stereotype by applying the predication to themselves, they simultaneously identify themselves within the referent as Asian. Whereas Anh willingly inhabits the stereotype, Sara is almost forced by Enoy who demands from her, "tell me your parents don't own anything in their life" (lines 92–95).

(12) Anh inhabits the stereotype

```
59    Anh:    I own a s- my parents own a store
```

(13) Sara inhabits the stereotype

```
97    Sara:   (?) in their life? they don't own anything
98            now, they did [but-
```

As Anh and Sara inhabit the stereotype, they also resist the stereotype. To signal resistance, Anh uses mostly paralinguistic cues, while Sara uses both paralinguistic and linguistic ones. Through her use of facial expressions, such as frowning and wrinkling her forehead downward (lines 53, 60–61, 68–69), Anh displays resistance and perhaps irritation toward Moeun's suggestion to write "owns a Chinese restaurant" (line 52) on the piece of paper. Sara, on the other hand, uses some gestures, such as slapping her pencil down (lines 104–106), but mostly uses denotationally explicit responses to resist scripting the Asian storeowner stereotype, for example, "they're not owning a restaurant" (line 88, 88–90), "you cannot do that" (lines 102–104), and "no (way)" (lines 104, 109). By performing these moves of resistance, Anh and Sara are also interactionally positioning themselves in opposition to others, particularly Moeun and Enoy, who support the relevance of the stereotype in their respective interactions.

While Anh and Sara display resistance, the other interactants use the stereotype as a resource for creating relationships with each other, as they interactionally position themselves as unified in support of the stereotype. In the first interaction, Didi ratifies Moeun's contribution, "owns a Chinese restaurant" (line 52), with "o::h okay yeah that's a good idea" (line 54). Kelly and Dan also align with Moeun by laughing with him and providing supporting information that "owns a Chinese restaurant" is appropriate to write on the outside of the head. When Moeun says, "cause like Asian people" (line 62), both Kelly and Dan collaborate with Moeun in the typifying of Asian Americans: Kelly says, "stereotypes" (line 63) and "grocery store" (line 67), and Dan says, "they always got to own something" (line 65). In the second interaction, after Jill suggests a line for the script, "like mom needs you at the store" (line 82), Enoy positions herself with respect to Jill as she agrees with her contribution, "all right ... mom needs you to watch the store" (lines 89–91). Moreover, Enoy and Jill, in one instance, jointly count types of stores that Asian Americans own, "nail salon, restaurant ... hair salon" (lines 113–116). Moeun, Didi, Kelly, and Dan, in the first interaction, and Enoy and Jill, in the second interaction, produce coherent discursive patterns as they align in terms of assessments (Goodwin & Goodwin, 1992)—joint laughter, cooperative completion of sentences, collaborative typification of Asian Americans—that interactionally position them as aligned with one another, while aligned against Anh and Sara, respectively.

Anh and Sara's resistance breaks, however, when Moeun and Enoy cohabit the stereotype with them. Coinhabiting created alignments between Anh and Moeun and between Sara and Enoy, which prevented Anh and Sara from being the sole inhabitors and targets of the stereotype.

(14) Moeun coinhabits the stereotype

```
70    Moeun:   my parents too heh heh
```

(15) Enoy coinhabits the stereotype

```
116   Enoy:   salon always (.) there's no joke- Manhattan
117           bagel (.) my uncle got a bagel store what the
118           hell is that? heh heh
```

When Moeun coinhabits the stereotype by admitting that his parents also own a store, Anh's resistance breaks. Anh seems pleased as she begins to smile (line 71), a facial signal new for her in this interaction. When Dan says, "drives minivan" (line 72), as another example of what others think of them, Moeun and Anh immediately align with each other. This is illustrated by their mutual eye gaze (lines 74, 77), simultaneous pointing toward Dan (lines 74, 77–78), and verbal agreement ("yeah" in lines 74, 75). Researchers argue that "gaze is not simply a means of obtaining information, the receiving end of a communication system, but is itself a social act" (C. Goodwin, 1981, p. 92). As Anh and Moeun gaze at each other, they are doing more than communicating; they are accomplishing a mutual orientation toward the invocation of Asian Americans driving minivans. Anh admits that her brother drives a minivan but does so with more humor and less resistance than when she inhabited the Asian storeowner stereotype. Laughter breaks through Anh's words as she says, "my brother drives (psycho) people to work every mo(hh)rning" (lines 79–80). Although owning a minivan may not seem to the outsider as relating to the topic of employment, it achieves such local meaning in this interaction. Anh's brother picks up Southeast Asian American workers on certain corners in South Philadelphia and drives them to work in the blueberry fields, garment factories, and other places of sweatshop labor. For this group of teens, owning a minivan is a narrowly circulating local typification that indexes low-income employment.

When Enoy coinhabits the stereotype by admitting "my uncle got a bagel store" (line 117), Sara's resistance also breaks. Rod and Jill join Enoy in laughter (lines 119–120) as the comic value of her inhabiting this stereotype may rely on the fact that her uncle owns a bagel store and not a Chinese restaurant, which has been listed as a typical occupation. Then, just as Anh's alignment shifted in the previous interaction after someone coinhabited the stereotype with her, Sara's alignment begins to shift as well. Sara ratifies Enoy's statement by uttering, "that's new that's new" (line 121), amid the laughter. Seemingly pleased that she was able to break Sara's resistance a little, Enoy smiles, raises her hand in front of Sara's face, and says, "they comin' up man" (lines 123–124). Finally, Sara, perhaps signaling that she has finally given up, places her head face down on the table (line 125).

Stereotypes as Oppressive Practice or Panethnic Resource

In addition to reappropriating stereotypes to position themselves and others in socially meaningful ways, the teens also constructed stereotyping as either an oppressive practice to resist or a panethnic resource to celebrate. When stereotyping was characterized as oppressive practice, it seemed an obvious resource for resisting mainstream homogenizing representations of Asian Americans as well as resisting attempts by participants within an interaction to homogenize Asian Americans. It is perhaps seen as acceptable to stereotype one's own ethnicity because a person is assumed to know more about his or her own ethnic group or because the person is seen as not being able to oppress his or her own (Chun, 2004). Yet as revealed by their anger and resistance, Anh and Sara interpreted others in the interaction as perpetuating stereotypes that served to oppress Asian Americans. In fact, Anh constructed stereotypes as oppressive because she perceived them as perpetuating only false things about Asians; she displayed confusion when stereotypes had elements of "truth." For instance, when Olive asked the teens why they had "minivan" written on their piece of paper, Anh said, "They think we drive minivans," then in a contemplative voice uttered, "But we do." Anh appeared to have a moment of confusion. She recognized that "they" thought the teens drove minivans, but she also noted that it was true for her and so was in the moment trying to figure out if true characterizations of behavior qualified as stereotypes. Unlike Anh, Sara seemed to argue that regardless if a stereotype was true or false, it was still "stereotypical" (line 104) and thus oppressive and homogenizing.

When stereotypes were characterized as panethnic resource, they became mechanisms for building social relationships and models with which to identify. As explained earlier, Moeun and Dan and Jill and Enoy constructed panethnic alliances that defended the relevance of a stereotype in their respective interactions. In addition, the teens collaboratively built stereotypes in ways that made them more accessible as resources with which to self- and other-identify. They did this by broadening a predication or reference so that it better applied to their experiences.

(16) Predication broadens from "owns a Chinese restaurant" to "owns a store"

```
52   Moeun:   oh (.) put owns a Chinese restaurant
53   Anh:     <turns lips down, wrinkles forehead downward>
54   Didi:    o::h ok[ay(.) yeah that's a good idea heh heh
55   Moeun:          [heh heh
56   Anh:     owns a store? <picks up marker>
57   Moeun:   yeah
```

(17) Reference broadens from "Chinese" to "Asian"

```
87    Jill:    a lot of Chinese people do own a restaurant
               ...
127   Rod:     Asian bagel store ha ha
```

Just as Van and Will broadened the ethnic scopes of Chinese martial arts and Vietnamese foods, these excerpts reveal how stereotypes are widened to become increasingly more applicable to interactants. After Moeun says, "put owns a Chinese restaurant" (line 52), Anh goes out of her way to make sure that Moeun also means "store" (line 56). By broadening the predication, Anh is able to construct the stereotype as applicable to her because her family owns a store, not a restaurant. In the second interaction, because the ethnicity of the characters in the working script was explicitly "Chinese," Jill typifies only Chinese people when she says, "a lot of Chinese people do own a restaurant" (line 87). But then Enoy applies this stereotype to her own experience by mentioning that her uncle, who is Cambodian Chinese American, owns a bagel store (line 117). As Rod says, "Asian bagel store" (line 127), he reveals that this stereotype has indeed widened to apply to Asian Americans, not just to Chinese Americans. These stereotypes, then, are formulated to be maximally applicable and available to the teens as meaningful resources with which to identify. By reconfiguring the ethnic scopes of stereotypes and applying stereotypes to their lives, these teens, like Van and Will, are producing an Asian American panethnicity in which they deliberately participate and locate themselves and each other.

Interactional Effects of Widespread Stereotypes Versus Local Typifications

When a widespread typification (e.g., Asian storeowner stereotype) was invoked in these two interactions, it brought about different interactional alignments and effects than those from a local typification (e.g., Asian minivan driver). Anh and Sara, who displayed resistance toward the widely circulating Asian storeowner stereotype, radically shifted their alignment after stereotypes were coinhabited and after local typifications, "drives minivan" (line 72) and "got a bagel store"[2] (line 117), were added in next-turn behavior. Both of these local typifications were contextualized with comic value by the subsequent laughter.

(18) Laughter after local typification: "drives minivan"

```
72    Dan:     drives minivan
73    Moeun:   heh heh
74    Anh:     o:h [yeah heh <gazes at Moeun, points to Dan>
75    Moeun:       [hell yeah hell [yeah if you don't drive=
76    Didi:                        [heh heh
77    Moeun:   =one you ain't Asian <gazes at Anh, points to
78             Dan> (1.9) drives minivan (4.6) heh heh
79    Anh:     my brother drives (psycho) people to work
80             every mo(hh)rning
81    Moeun:   heh heh
```

(19) Laughter after local typification: "got a bagel store"

```
116   Enoy:    salon always (.) there's no joke- Manhattan
117            bagel (.) my uncle got a bagel store what the
118            hell is that? heh heh
119   Rod:     [heh heh
120   Jill:    [heh heh
```

These local typifications were critical in breaking the interactional frame (Goffman, 1974) from serious resistance to comic event, which resulted in Anh's compliance and Sara's surrender. As noted earlier, Anh and Sara interpreted the widely circulating Asian storeowner stereotype as oppressive and homogenizing. Local typifications, on the other hand, may have been seen as novel, innocuous, and not in need of active resistance, because their circulation was restricted to local interactions among Asian Americans who found them humorous. Constructing a common identity as they indexed in-group knowl-

---

[2]Owning a bagel store may not technically qualify as a local typification, because a bagel store is still a store and can fall under the Asian storeowner stereotype. However, the atypical ownership of a bagel store, as illustrated by Enoy's "what the hell is that?" (lines 113–116), as opposed to the typical ownership of a "nail salon, restaurant … hair salon" (lines 115–116) is what I am emphasizing as not widespread.

edge, these local typifications functioned to create a sense of community by distinguishing between those who knew this local "fact" about Asian Americans from outsiders who did not. The teens displayed no resistance to a local typification perhaps because it was within their control; communities outside of their own were unaware of it and thus could not use it against the teens as they went about the world. If "Asian minivan driver" began to circulate widely in a societal speech chain network (Agha, 2003), however, it might have no longer generated laughter among participants because it would have no longer functioned to index in-group knowledge. Instead, the image of the Asian minivan driver would have become another stereotype to contend with and also another stereotype to reappropriate as an interactional resource.

CONCLUSION

This chapter reveals how notions of race, ethnicity, and panethnicity operate not only as organizing principles at the level of large-scale social groups but also as local and flexible achievements at the level of interaction. Discourse analysis exposed the intricate ways in which Asian American panethnicity was constructed through conversations in which Asian American stereotypes were invoked. Problematizing essentialized notions of race and ethnicity, the teenagers at the video-making project reconfigured stereotypes to be maximally available as resources with which to build their identities and create a sense of panethnic community. For example, while Van as Vietnamese American interactionally inhabited the Chinese martial arts expert stereotype and Will as Chinese American claimed Vietnamese foods as culturally familiar to him, they redrew ethnic boundaries in the production of an Asian American panethnicity in which they both located themselves.

Panethnic Asian American community was also formed as teens invoked the widely circulating stereotype of the Asian storeowner. As teens positioned themselves and others in relation to this stereotype, they revealed how stereotypes can be used to resist oppressive practices, form social relationships, celebrate a means of identifying, provoke laughter, and build panethnicity. In both interactions, Anh and Sara's positions of resistance were temporary and shifted according to how these social actions unfolded and related to one another. Whether teens used stereotypes to resist others and homogenizing representations of Asian Americans or to celebrate a panethnic identity together in opposition to others, the teens revealed how stereotypes were resources with which to identify and construct oneself, others, and connections between individuals and groups.

What seemed to be occurring was the production of an Asian American panethnicity that was licensed to legitimately claim multiple ethnic and cultural elements in its heterogeneous formation. As members of panethnic Asian American friendship groups, eating panethnic Asian foods and participating in a panethnic Asian American community arts organization, the teens actively participated in social practices and relationships across ethnic groups. Through the reappropriation of Asian American stereotypes at the level of local interaction, the teens revealed the possibilities of transgressing ethnic boundaries in the formation of panethnic community. Both Asian Americans and non-Asian Americans may foster such Asian American panethnicity, though from different ideological positions. Whereas U.S. institutions promote a view of Asian Americans as a homogeneous mass of forever foreigners or model minorities, Asian Americans generally view themselves as a heterogeneous group. The panethnic Asian American movement promotes panethnicity, not to erase the differences between and within Asian American ethnic groups but to build coalitions for political mobilization (Espiritu, 1992).

As opposed to melting into one homogeneous Asian American community, the teens may have promoted a heterogeneous panethnicity that allowed for the reconfiguration of ethnic boundaries. However, the teens also actively maintained ethnic boundaries, particularly when the Other Asian identity was foregrounded as separate from the experiences of other Asian Americans. The next chapter explores this issue by examining the ways in which the Southeast Asian American teenagers sometimes rejected Asian American panethnicity and instead highlighted distinctions among Asian American ethnic groups.

5

"Yo, Yo, He Cambo": Dismantling Panethnicity With Asian American Stereotypes

We got Chinatown. Where the Cambo-town? Laos-town?
—Enoy, 2001

In contrast to locating themselves within a panethnic Asian American community, the Southeast Asian American teenagers sometimes established ethnic boundaries to differentiate themselves from other Asian American ethnic groups. Part of the motivation for fixing ethnic lines was the reported inability of non-Asians to recognize different Asian ethnicities. According to the teens, non-Asians not only often assumed that they were Chinese, Japanese, or Korean but also sometimes admitted to never having heard of Cambodians, Vietnamese, or Laotians before meeting them. Many teens saw the video-making project as a means to remedy this situation. With the goal of presenting their lives for public consumption, the teens were actively engaged in increasing the ethnic recognizability of the Other Asian, distinguishing their experiences from other Asian American ethnic groups.

In the opening quote, Enoy (Cambodian Chinese American female) offered yet another way to increase the visibility of the Other Asian: lay claim to public spaces. She explained that whereas Chinese Americans had Chinatown, Cambodian and Laotian Americans did not have designated areas of Philadelphia named after them. As opposed to perceiving Chinatown as representing a site for Asian American panethnic community, Enoy constructed Chinatown as separate from Southeast Asian Americans, whom she felt deserved areas of their own. One exception was a small section of South Philadelphia locally known as

"Khmer Street," a two-block strip of a few Cambodian American small businesses near which several teens also lived. Yet whereas most Philadelphians knew of Chinatown, Khmer Street was generally only known among Southeast Asian Americans in Philadelphia and among those who lived on neighboring blocks. Public recognition of designated city spaces for Southeast Asian Americans and public consumption of their videos were just two of many proposals offered by the teens for increasing the ethnic recognizability of the Other Asian.

The teens linked issues of ethnic recognizability not only to ethnic group distinctions but also to concepts of culture. As 1.5 and second generation Southeast Asian Americans, the teens were frequently perceived as caught between two cultural binaries: Southeast Asia and the United States. Yet oftentimes the teens were seen as more Americanized and thus accused of "losing their culture." When discussing their family relationships at the video-making project, for example, the teens often claimed that their parents—who formed informal community watchdog groups—kept a close eye on them and their Southeast Asian American peers who engaged in so-called American behaviors, such as sexual relationships, gang affiliation, disrespect to elders, and school truancy. Adult family and community members were not the only ones who reportedly expressed these views about the teens. Teachers, advisors, and administrators of several different ethnic backgrounds—including Asian American, European American, and African American—also evaluated the teens as losing their culture after attending screenings of the teen-created videos, particularly the 1999 video *American Sroksrei*, which depicted romantic relationships, drug use, gang life, and hip hop culture.

Even the teens sometimes subscribed to these binary oppositions. In a radio interview with a reporter who was working on a story about community video making, Sokla (Cambodian American male) stated, "Growing up, it's kind of hard in America, seeing like your own customs and your American customs really don't match up." Although this cultural binary perspective was prevalent, there were also moments when the teens disrupted this paradigm by constructing culture in new ways. The Southeast Asian American teenagers sometimes linked concepts of cultural value to ethnic recognizability, creating a new definition of culture that involved others taking responsibility for recognizing the Other Asian as distinct from other Asian American groups.

Focusing on issues of ethnic recognizability and cultural value, this chapter reveals how stereotypes were used not only to create panethnicity but also to dismantle it. The stereotype that the teens mostly responded to here was "all Asians are Chinese": that when people encounter someone of seemingly Asian descent, they assume that the person is Chinese (or Japanese or Korean) because images of East Asian ethnic groups circulate more widely in U.S. society. In this chapter, I explore how the teens at the video-making project discussed how they and others differentially recognized and evaluated Asian American ethnic groups, particularly along generational lines, at the expense of a unified panethnic formation. I also closely analyze an interaction in which Southeast Asian American teens and non-Asian adults constructed two distinct schemas of culture: "culture as historical transmission" and "culture as emblem of ethnic differentiation," the latter of which reveals how stereotypes about ethnic recognizability intersect with ideas about cultural value, resulting in the obstruction of panethnic community. This chapter examines how broad notions of culture and ethnicity emerge from interaction, revealing how flexible and multidimensional these concepts are. Because the teens used stereotypes to argue for the increased recognizability of the Other Asian, they sometimes foregrounded ethnic distinctions as opposed to ethnic unity in the momentary deconstruction of Asian American panethnicity.

CIRCULATION OF CULTURE AND ETHNICITY

The concept of culture has been interrogated from several different theoretical perspectives and methodological approaches. Historically connoting a wide range of broad definitions from "civilization" to "the everyday" to "high art" (Williams, 1976), culture has more recently been understood as locally grounded in contextually bound social practices (Duranti, 1997). Silverstein and Urban (1996), for example, emphasized that culture cannot be analyzed as a collection of texts apart from their contextual surrounds; rather, culture can only be examined as ongoing processes within social orders. The perspective I use in this chapter is one that views language as central to cultural process because communication comprises a large part of how people come into contact with cultural forms and values (see Duranti, 1997, for a survey of theories of culture). With this emphasis on situated language use, research in linguistic anthropology reveals how culture is both created and reproduced through social interaction. Although culture exists by virtue of its being invoked in interaction, culture also provides the necessary framework for interpreting interaction (Silverstein, 1998). Moreover, culture is not limited to one local moment but is somehow socially shared and recognized at the level of groups, reproduced and modified in other interactions across time and space (Silverstein, 1998). Accepting that culture is not a thing but a process, researchers face the problem of placing such a slippery concept under empirical scrutiny.

Almost directly responding to such a challenge, contemporary linguistic anthropology has been at the theoretical forefront, moving the field toward a circulatory account of culture (Agha, 2003; Bauman & Briggs, 1990; Silverstein & Urban, 1996; Urban, 2001). Particularly interested in how cultural values circulate in society, Agha (2003) argued that culture is observable in social practice rather than fixed in the minds of members of cultural groups. He asserted that discursive practices assign recognizable values to cultural forms while bringing these values into circulation among speakers. Thus, a circulatory account of culture obliges researchers to analyze how cultural messages are transmitted across society through communicative means. This model of circulation is envisioned in terms of senders and receivers of cultural messages within speech chain networks.[1] Senders and receivers need not have direct contact with one another but are part of a common discursive history. For example, later in this chapter I discuss how the phrase "all means all" was taken up by a speaker as the motto of liberal multiculturalism. The person who initially authored these words and the person who animated (Goffman, 1981) them later most likely did not know each other, yet they belonged to the same speech chain that widely circulated this message of valuing cultural diversity.

Similarly, when dealing with ethnicity, the recognizability of ethnic groups such as Chinese or Laotian Americans relies on their circulation in speech chain networks. Perhaps not surprisingly, the image of Chinese Americans, the Asian ethnic group in the United States with the longest history (Takaki, 1989) and largest population (Barnes & Bennett, 2002), circulates more widely in mass media than that of Laotian Americans, an Asian ethnic group that was largely absent from the American ethnic landscape prior to their mass immigration waves beginning in 1975 (Niedzwiecki & Duong, 2004). In this chapter, I examine how the speech chain that circulated the value of cultural diversity intersects with the speech chain that circulated Southeast Asian ethnic groups, re-

---

[1]See chapter 1 for an extended discussion of speech chain networks.

sulting in the production of a link between the issue of cultural maintenance and the recognizability of ethnic groups.

Ethnic Kinds

Throughout this chapter, I explore how the Southeast Asian American teenagers at the after-school video-making project often constructed themselves as ethnically distinct at the expense of a panethnic Asian American formation. Drawing on the work of Putnam (1975), I extend his discussion of natural kinds to ethnic kinds and apply it to how the Southeast Asian American teenagers argued for their increased ethnic recognizability. Putnam claimed that entities such as water and tigers are natural kinds, whereas objects such as elm trees and gold require a linguistic division of labor. In regard to the latter, he argued that even though most people have acquired the word "gold," they need experts to tell them whether gold is real or not. Similarly, with an elm tree, people may understand that an elm is a tree, which is a necessary condition, but this understanding falls short of constituting a way of recognizing elms, of fixing their extension. The extension of gold or elm thus relies on a linguistic division of labor by a collective linguistic body consisting of those who simply acquire the term and those who are gold and tree experts.

Natural kinds, on the other hand, do not require linguistic divisions of labor but can be fully acquired in two ways. First, an ostensive definition involves the speaker indicating an explicit or implicit marker and saying, for example, "this is water." Putnam (1975) provides an overview of the second way, description:

> [Description] typically consists of one or more markers together with a stereotype—a standardized description of features of the kind that are typical, or "normal", or at any rate stereotypical. The central features of the stereotype generally are criteria—features which in normal situations constitute ways of recognizing if a thing belongs to the kind or, at least, necessary conditions (or probabilistic necessary conditions) for membership in the kind. (p. 230)

According to Putnam (1975), a tiger is a natural kind. To describe a tiger, a person might use an ostensive definition by simply pointing to a picture of a tiger and saying to a child, "This is a tiger." An ostensive definition such as this may be sufficient enough for the child to identify tigers from that moment on. In addition to using a marker, however, a person may employ a stereotype such as "tigers are orange with black stripes." But unlike a term that requires a linguistic division of labor, a natural kind term generally enables people to recognize objects without the need of experts.

Extending the notion of natural kinds to ethnic kinds, I examine something that emerged as extremely important among the Southeast Asian American teenagers at the after-school video-making project. In the following sections, I explore how the teens did not want their ethnicity to require a linguistic division of labor, where people would have to rely on ethnicity experts to help them ethnically identify the teens. Rather, the teens wanted their ethnicity to be a natural kind—or ethnic kind—where everyday individuals by themselves could recognize Southeast Asian American ethnic groups without mistaking them for more widely circulating Asian American ethnic groups, such as Chinese, Japanese, and Korean Americans. Yet because the recognizability of ethnic groups relies on their circulation in speech chain networks, Southeast Asian ethnic groups are left largely unrecognizable by mainstream Americans because they do not circulate in discourse as widely as East Asian ethnic groups.

ETHNIC RECOGNIZABILITY

Most, if not all, of the teens at the video-making project agreed that Chinese and Japanese ethnic groups were typically the only Asian American groups depicted on television and in film. The relative absence of Southeast Asian Americans from circulation in entertainment media, they argued, led mainstream Americans to believe that all Asians are Chinese, thus incapable of recognizing Southeast Asian ethnic groups as distinct ethnic kinds. From the perspective of both the Asian Arts Initiative and the teen participants, one of the main goals of the video-making project was to increase the recognizability of Southeast Asian Americans by showcasing the diversity of Asian American experiences, in regard not only to ethnicities but also to socioeconomic statuses, genders, languages, generations, immigration histories, and so on. The teens were acutely aware of the many differences between Asian American ethnic groups and often highlighted these differences at the expense of a unified panethnic Asian American formation.

Ethnic Epithets

The Southeast Asian American teenagers often linked the topic of ethnic epithets to issues of ethnic recognizability and panethnicity. Two of the most common ethnic slurs that the teens identified were "chink" and "gook." Similar to other derisive labels based on categories of race and ethnicity, such as "nigger" (Kennedy, 2002), chink and gook are also typically used by out-group members to scornfully refer to those perceived as members of the targeted group. Whereas chink is a derogatory label originally used by non-Asians against Chinese people, gook is often thought to have initially been used by American soldiers to express contempt for Koreans during the Korean War, but it is now also associated with the Vietnamese, again as a result of war. Both ethnic epithets have been applied to Asian American ethnic groups other than Chinese, Korean, and Vietnamese Americans, partly as a result of discourses, which create a monolithic image of Asian Americans that elide the heterogeneity within this racial formation (Lowe, 1996). That is, perceptions of racial homogeneity invite ethnic epithets to be applied to all members of a racial group, reflecting the "all Asians look alike" or "all Asians are Chinese" stereotypes, the latter of which results from Chinese images circulating more widely in U.S. society than images of other Asian ethnic groups.

The teens linked the inability of non-Asians to recognize their ethnic identities with the issue of ethnic epithets. In the following interaction, ethnic slurs are discussed during a project session in 2001 in which small groups of teens with the help of adult volunteers wrote what others think about them on a large piece of paper. The interaction begins as an adult volunteer, Kelly (Vietnamese American female), asks the teens in her group—Moeun, Dan (Cambodian Chinese American males), and Anh (Vietnamese Cambodian Chinese American female)—whether people misconstrue their ethnic identities.

(1)

```
1    Kelly:   do people ever mistaken like- um- your
2             ethnicities?
3    Moeun:   yeah Korean
4    Anh:     they always call me chink, or whatever
5    Moeun:   I know they always call me something else
6    Anh:     where should I write chink
```

```
7    Moeun:    they think I'm Chinese
8    Anh:      um chink, gook <writing>
9    Dan:      it's 'cause you're Asian, automatically
10             Chinese
11   Anh:      is that how you spell gook
```

Moeun, Anh, and Dan discuss how they are prevented from being recognized as ethnic kinds because of the "all Asians are Chinese" stereotype: "it's 'cause you're Asian, automatically Chinese" (lines 9–10). They argue that others misidentify them for more widely circulating ethnic groups, such as "Korean" (line 3) and "Chinese" (lines 7, 10), sometimes through the use of ethnic slurs, such as "chink" (line 4) and "gook" (line 8). Yet Chinese and Korean ethnicities do not emerge as ethnic kinds either because people are characterized as incorrectly assuming that the teens are of Chinese or Korean descent. This reflects the "all Asians look alike" racial homogenization of Asian Americans. Interestingly, although all three teens are part Chinese, when they are called Chinese, Moeun sees it as something other than himself (lines 5, 7), perhaps viewing a "true" Chinese person as one who is not ethnically mixed or one who is from China, unlike the teens whose families immigrated from Southeast Asian countries. Nevertheless, misidentification and verbal abuse become intertwined issues for Moeun, Anh and Dan. Other teens also conveyed similar experiences: For example, Ny (Vietnamese Laotian Cambodian American female) complained about being called "chinks, gooks and stuff," and Chea (Cambodian Vietnamese Chinese American male) reported that non-Asians sometimes walked up to him and said, "ching, chong, chang," as if speaking Chinese. These perspectives reflected a desire to be recognized as distinct from Chinese and Korean Americans, to be ungrouped from East Asian Americans and removed from a panethnic formation.

The teens, however, also reappropriated ethnic epithets, momentarily stripping them of their derogatory connotations in certain contexts. For example, some teens called each other chink as a term of solidarity, similar to the way that African Americans have reappropriated "nigga" (Kennedy, 2002) and gay communities have reappropriated "queer" (Jagose, 1997). Bao (Cambodian American male) even proudly claimed that his nickname was "Chink." That he and other teens were not of Chinese descent did not prevent them from claiming and applying this ethnic-specific Chinese label for their own positive use. In this sense, chink achieved panethnic use. For instance, one day when Lena (Chinese

Cambodian Vietnamese American female), Tommy (Cambodian American male), and I were talking in my office at the Asian Arts Initiative, Lena and Tommy began playfully teasing each other and she called him chink. They continued laughing and he said "cambo-soup," a local term of solidarity among Cambodian Americans created from a pun on "Cambo" (short for "Cambodian") and the Campbell Soup Company. That the ethnic labels—chink and cambo-soup—were used consecutively in the same jocular interaction without a change in key (Goffman, 1974) suggests that the term "chink" not only became momentarily devoid of its offensive baggage when spoken among Asian Americans but also served as a creative resource for establishing a playful interactional context in which social relationships were fostered among fellow Asian American youth.

Yet there were also moments when the teens applied ethnic epithets to other Asian Americans in a derogatory manner, particularly when creating divisions of identity within ethnic groups. Unlike when the teens playfully applied ethnic epithets panethnically, here the teens used them to dismantle panethnicity. For example, during one project session in 2002, Macy (Vietnamese American female) used the term "gook" as a resource for distancing herself from other Vietnamese Americans. On this day, Will (Chinese American male) was telling a small group of teens that he liked Chinese rap music. Macy then told a story about a group of Vietnamese American students who performed a Vietnamese rap song at her high school talent show. She said, "I'm not stereotyping, but they're gook," then complained that the Vietnamese rappers were a negative representation of "us," perhaps indexing herself and other Vietnamese Americans who were not "gook." Thus, ethnic epithets were sometimes used to divide Asian American identities, hindering the formation of panethnic community.

Ethnic Pride

Macy further argued that the Vietnamese rappers at her high school talent show exhibited "Viet pride," which, like "Asian pride," was often negatively evaluated by the teens at the video-making project. Exhibiting Asian or ethnic pride by, for example, rapping in Vietnamese, contributes to the increased ethnic recognizability of one's ethnic kind. Though the Southeast Asian American teens were aligned with the goal of increasing ethnic recognizability, many teens at the video-making project claimed that those with Asian or ethnic pride not only thought that they were better than other racial or ethnic groups but also were generally unwilling to socialize outside of their respective race or ethnicity. Although the teens at the video-making project came together in an explicitly panethnic Asian American organization to create videos about their lives as Asian Americans, they did not tend to view themselves as ethnic separatists or as superior to other racial or ethnic groups. Because they generally formed friendship groups across ethnic and racial lines, the teens, on the one hand, criticized others' disregard for panethnic formation, yet, on the other hand, deconstructed panethnicity and even ethnicity by, for example, extracting "gooks" from "us."

Such dismantling of panethnicity in the name of panethnicity was also found in the construction of Korean Americans as the ultimate possessors of ethnic pride. Many teens often accused Korean Americans of having superiority complexes and of refusing to mingle with other Asian American ethnic groups. Stacey Lee (1996) also found that many Southeast Asian American students in her study thought the Korean-identified students were arrogant; in fact, the Korean students often explicitly claimed to be superior to other Asian Americans. In the following interaction from a scriptwriting session in 2001, Enoy (Cambodian Chinese American female), Jill (Haitian Cuban American female), Sara (Chinese American female), and Cindy (Chinese Burmese American female) discuss interethnic tensions between Korean and Japanese Americans.

(2)

```
12   Enoy:    nobody gets along with Koreans though
13   Jill:    yeah
14   Enoy:    see- [see-
15   Sara:         [don't they stay by themselves I guess
16   Enoy:    yeah- yeah they are
17   Jill:    they're always by themselves
18   Cindy:   yeah they are
19   Enoy:    I be gettin' ma:d I be like what you do-
```

After Enoy states "nobody gets along with Koreans" (line 12), Jill (lines 13, 17), Sara (line 15), and Cindy (line 18) explicitly agree that Korean Americans "stay by themselves" (line 15). The teens build consensus on the issue of Korean American segregation practices, practices that Enoy finds particularly aggravating: "I be gettin' mad" (line 19). Because the participants in this interaction ethnically identified as Cambodian Chinese, Haitian Cuban, Chinese, and Chinese Burmese, they describe Korean Americans as something the teens were not, that is, unwilling to interact in multiethnic peer groups. Associating exclusively with those who claim the same ethnicity—as Korean Americans were characterized as doing—was consistently negatively evaluated by the teens, while fostering friendships across ethnic groups was often positively evaluated. Lena (Chinese Cambodian Vietnamese American female), for example, explicitly stated that she did not want to associate only with Chinese Americans or even Asian Americans; instead, she said she preferred to have a "mixed" peer group.

Not only did non-Korean American teens express such views about Korean Americans but so did one Korean American teen at the video-making project. In the first 3 years of the after-school video-making project, there were no Korean American teens, but in the last year, there was Choi, a second generation Korean American female, and Eva, a Korean-born female adoptee with European American parents. Choi once stated, "I don't want to stereotype, but most Koreans are traditional and have Korean pride that they throw in your face." Choi's negative perception of Korean ethnic pride emerged during a project session in 2002 when she was part of a small group that had to create a story with two characters. Bart (Chinese American male), who was also in her group, suggested that they make one character Korean American and the other Japanese American because "Koreans hate Japanese." Choi agreed, saying that Korean Americans "still hold a grudge" against the Japanese because of the atrocities of World War II. After Choi and the other teens in her small group took up Bart's suggestion to create Japanese and Korean American characters, they discussed what generation they should be. They chose to create a first generation Korean American male character and a third generation Japanese American female character. They argued that because first generation Korean Americans were more "traditional," the Korean American character would have developed a hatred for the Japanese. Because the teens claimed that a third generation Japanese American "does not care about ethnicity" and is not "conservative like first generation," the teens thought that the meeting of these two characters would create an interesting conflict in their story. Choi added that the Korean American character should act like he is wealthy because all Korean Americans do, but she wanted his parents to own a self-service laundry so that he is only pretending to be rich. After the project session, Lena told me that "Choi hates Korean guys, badmouthing Koreans and *she's* Korean." As antagonism toward Korean Americans circulated strongly at the video-making project, Choi explicitly distanced herself from other Korean Americans and instead aligned herself with the teens at the video-making project, who also negatively evaluated ethnic pride in favor of panethnic community.

Yet by disparaging members of ethnic kinds with ethnic pride, the teens created a generational division of identity that partly deconstructed panethnicity. Although the teens criticized Asian Americans with ethnic pride for separating themselves from other ethnic groups, the teens simultaneously separated themselves from those with ethnic pride, which served to hinder panethnic formation. The teens linked issues of ethnic pride with other locally meaningful categories, such as generation, memory, tradition, and conservatism, and created divisions within ethnic groups according to how these categories aligned with one another. What resulted was an explicit division between the 1.5 and second generation teens at the video-making project and first generation Asian Americans, who were constructed as having ethnic pride. I argue that Choi's negative assessment of fellow Korean Americans was linked to Macy's negative assessment of fellow Vietnamese Americans, both of which were also linked to the Asian American teens' negative assessment of fellow Asian Americans as "F.O.B."[2] In all three cases, the relevant division of identity emerged not along ethnic or racial lines but along generational lines: Negatively evaluated Korean Americans, Vietnamese Americans, and Asian Americans were all first generation. The teens thus attended to generation, not ethnicity, as the locally meaningful division of identity, which functioned to thwart their own efforts at building panethnic Asian American community.

Ethnic Harmony and Discord

The teens discussed not only the interethnic and intraethnic tensions between themselves and first generation Asian Americans with ethnic pride but also the interethnic affinities between certain Asian American groups. Such conversations about ethnic harmony and discord among Asian American ethnic groups also revealed the possibilities and pitfalls of panethnicity. Although panethnic identity was foregrounded when discussing inter-ethnic accord, the persistent

---

[2]See chapter 2 for an extensive discussion of this third ethnic epithet, an initialism for "Fresh Off the Boat," which the teens often used as a derogatory label for newly arrived Asian immigrants.

concern over interethnic conflict deconstructed Asian American panethnic formation. Such keen awareness of the differences among Asian American ethnic
groups also revealed the importance of ethnic recognizability: If one could not
recognize different ethnic groups, then one could not understand the local divisions of identity that were socially meaningful.

Such issues of ethnic harmony and discord are vividly revealed in the following interaction at a scriptwriting session for the 2001 video. The week before
this interaction, the teen scriptwriters decided to create an African American
male character because they wanted to make the video about racial tensions
between Asian Americans and African Americans. As the video-making project
coordinator that year, I had to intervene and inform the adult scriptwriting artist,
Didi (Indian American female), that we could not script an African American
male character because the teen participants had to be the actors in the video,
and there were no African American males in the group. I offered a few suggestions: They could still make a video about interracial tension by scripting a
Black female character instead and have Jill (Haitian Cuban American female),
the only non-Asian participant at the video-making project, play the role, or they
could make a video about interethnic tension between Asian American ethnic
groups. The following interaction begins after the teen scriptwriters—Jill, Enoy
(Cambodian Chinese American female), Rod (Laotian American male), and
Sara (Chinese American female)—decided that they wanted to revise the story
so that it would be about Asian American interethnic conflict between Ny, the
female character, and a male character who was yet unnamed.

(3)

```
20   Didi:   so: could it be like uh: (0.7) Chinese and
21           Cambodian? is that a-?
22   Enoy:   no no, Chinese and Cambodian get along too::
23           well
24   Didi:   oh really heh heh
25   Sara:   heh heh
26   Enoy:   if you- if you ask Cambodian person, are you
27           mixed, are you pure, oh I'm mixed Chinese, a
28           lot of Chinese people be like oh I'm mixed
29           Cambodian
```

Simply by asking if there are tensions between Chinese and Cambodian Americans (lines 20–21), Didi positions herself as an outsider to this group of teens. Enoy then depicts Chinese and Cambodian Americans not only as distinct ethnic kinds in harmony with one another (lines 22–23) but also as frequently ethnically mixed together (lines 26–29). Enoy, who identified as "mixed Cambodian Chinese," was living proof of this. As the interaction continues, Didi asks the teens about how their parents would react if they dated an Asian American outside of their respective ethnic groups, which provokes Enoy to discuss interethnic tensions.

(4)

```
30   Didi:    like think of your own families like what do
31            your- your parents get. in- in your own
32            families if you have- if you were dating
33            someone from anoth- who's Asian but he's from
34            another or she's [from another-
35   Enoy:                    [no but then like- I don't
36            know about anyone else be saying, but my mom
37            and dad? they would get all hostile if I was
38            going out with a- um Vietnamese guy or
39            something-
```

Prompted by Didi's question, Enoy reveals an ethnic conflict between her family and Vietnamese Americans. Vietnamese Americans emerge as an ethnic kind—alongside Chinese and Cambodian Americans—as Enoy explains that her parents would not accept her dating a Vietnamese American (lines 37–38). Perhaps at this moment Didi has become privy to the local interethnic tension that circulates among the teens. As the interaction continues, however, Didi reveals that she has not yet fully comprehended which Asian American ethnic group is in conflict with Vietnamese Americans.

(5)

```
40   Didi:    s- so uh: if you make the- if so- wha- wha-
41            what- if you make Ny, can you make Ny Chinese?
42            and uh: dating a Vietnamese man?
43   Sara:    yeah
```

```
44   Didi:   d- do you think that'll be-
45   Enoy:   why don't she be Cambodian
46   Jill:   t ha ha ha ha ha
47   Rod:    ha ha ha ha
48   Enoy:   no cause- it's Cambodian people that don't get
49           along with Vietnamese people
50   Didi:   oh really?
51   Enoy:   yeah
```

Building from Enoy's story about interethnic conflict between her family and Vietnamese Americans, Didi suggests that the female character in the video, Ny, be Chinese American and the male character be Vietnamese American (lines 41–42). Didi's suggestion exposes a presupposition: that Enoy's Chinese ethnic identity—not her Cambodian ethnic identity—is the one that is in conflict with Vietnamese Americans. Sara, who is Chinese American, expresses agreement with Didi's suggestion (line 43), but Enoy rejects it and asserts that it is Cambodian and Vietnamese Americans who are in conflict with one another. Jill and Rod's laughter (lines 46–47) may be in response to Enoy's repeated efforts to reject Didi's suggestions and assert her own opinions (lines 22, 45). A few moments later in the interaction, Enoy reveals why this interethnic tension exists.

(6)

```
52   Enoy:   Viet- Vietnamese soldiers took over the
53           country. they took over Ca- Cambodia, that's
54           why Cambodian parents, the o:lder people they
55           gettin' all hostile about Vietnamese people,
56           see if it was us kids we don't really care,
57           but it's the- the older heads
58   Rod:    old heads
```

Just as it did in the previous section on ethnic pride, generation emerges as a relevant division of identity that obstructs Asian American panethnic formation. Enoy explains the historical circumstances that continue to influence interethnic conflict between Cambodian and Vietnamese Americans. She claims that these tensions exist primarily among the older generation but not the younger generation of "us kids" (line 56). The scriptwriters decided to follow Enoy's suggestion: The female character, later renamed Moi, was Cambodian American, and the male character, later named Hoa, was Vietnamese American. The story they created for the video *Ba. Bay. Three.* depicted Moi and Hoa in an interethnic romance that was met with disapproval from Moi's family. When the video was screened at an Asian American teen event at the Asian Arts Initiative the following fall, I asked several teen viewers about the representation of Cambodian and Vietnamese Americans. They unanimously agreed that the interethnic tension portrayed in the story was accurate. Such videos and the interactions that produced them contributed to the ethnic recognizability of the Other Asian not only by depicting Cambodian and Vietnamese Americans as distinct ethnic kinds but also by revealing the differences between and within them. Offering rare and complex visions of Asian American communities, the teens helped debunk myths of racial homogeneity and the stereotype that "all Asians are Chinese." By creating such stories of ethnic conflict, the teens both undermined and reinforced panethnicity. That is, the teens partly inhibited the formation of Asian American panethnic community by highlighting divisions across ethnic and generational lines and partly supported the formation of panethnicity because the video ultimately expressed hopes for interethnic harmony.

CULTURAL VALUE

The topic of ethnic recognizability also emerges in conjunction with the issue of cultural value. In this section, I explore how they function together to deconstruct Asian American panethnicity as well. I analyze an interaction to illustrate how culture emerges as two constructs: "culture as historical transmission" and "culture as emblem of ethnic differentiation," the latter of which reveals how cultural value intersects with the recognizability of Southeast Asian Americans as ethnic kinds. These schemas are accomplished, in part, through emergent indexical patterns that shape categories and trajectories of personae to which speech event participants are recruited. I argue that these two schemas of culture are not merely static essences but are dynamically linked to distinct participation frameworks that achieve particular performative effects. These schemas brought forth into circulation reveal how macrolevel constructs, such as culture and ethnicity, are played out rather vividly in microlevel interaction.

The Speech Event

The interaction I analyze in this chapter occurred during the School District of Philadelphia's "All Means All, Diversity and Equity Issues and Solutions in Education" conference in spring 2000.[3] The school district invited the teens from the video-making project to present a workshop in which they would discuss their experiences in an after-school program at a community arts organization and screen the teen-created video from the year before (the 2000 video was still in progress). The discourse excerpts presented here are from the discussion between the teen panel and the audience members after the audience viewed the 1999 video *American Sroksrei*. The five Asian American teens on the conference panel were Moeun (Cambodian Chinese American male); Loc, Theth, and Boi (Cambodian American males); and Yem (Cambodian Chinese American female). I was the panel moderator. There were 27 audience members, most of whom were teachers, advisors, and administrators from the school district, including Nicole (European American female), Joe (African American male), Kim (African American female), and Sapna (Indian American female), who was a school district administrator and member of the Asian Arts Initiative. In addition, three Asian Arts Initiative staff members were present in the audience. Finally, there was also one unidentified female audience member, referred to as Amy, who appeared in the interaction.

Denotational Text, Interactional Text, and Indexicality

Before analyzing the interaction, I briefly review some principles of discourse analysis that are applied to the excerpts. Several of these concepts were introduced and applied in previous chapters, but I discuss them again here, particularly with attention to how they inform the analysis. First, Silverstein (1993) used the terms "denotational text" and "interactional text" to refer to two types of coherence that discursive interaction can be taken to manifest. The denotational text is a coherent representation of content, the subject matter under discussion in a given interaction. In the interactional text, a recognizable interaction coheres as the speech event participants, namely the speaker and audience, are positioned in socially meaningful ways as particular types of people. In a dia-

---

[3]The School District of Philadelphia granted me permission to identify the name of the school district and title of the conference.

logic approach to language, Bakhtin (1935/1981) claimed that these two types of textuality depend on each other for their meaningfulness. To construe this meaning, I turn to work in indexicality.

Indexical patterns collectively presuppose certain contextual aspects as most relevant to an interaction. The meaning of indexicals—such as "we" and "this"—is indecipherable without appeal to the situation of utterance. Thus, indexical forms rely on both surrounding cotext (what is said before and after) and context (aspects of the situation) for their meaningfulness, while making salient particular aspects of cotext and context (Benveniste, 1954/1971; Peirce, 1932; Silverstein, 1976, 1998). In the analysis of the panel discussion, the second schema of culture emerges as participants use pronominal indexicals such as "us" and "them" as well as nonpronominal indexicals such as "Cambodians" and "people" to create groups and draw boundaries between them. Speech event participants, namely, the members of the panel and the audience, are then recruited to these indexically invoked categories. This process contributes to the interactional positioning of individuals as they are assigned to the groups that are denotationally constituted.

Culture as Historical Transmission

About 15 min into the panel discussion, the first schema of culture emerges when Nicole (European American female), an adult audience member, asks the following question. Prior to this excerpt, teens were describing how boys and girls in their families are treated differently and how the video addresses these concerns.

(7)

```
59   Nicole:  what happens to families as- if- if you're in
60            Americ- a- are y- w- all of y- were born- in-
61            your countries? or
```

Both temporal and spatial dimensions are laid out as a frame by Nicole's utterance. That is, there are the temporal distinctions between the present tense "you're in America" (you *are*) and the past tense "y- *were* born- in- your countries," along with the spatial distinctions between "America" and "your countries." Thus, the spatiotemporal dimensions of current residence in "America" and past birthplace in "your countries" emerge as meaningful distinctions in the question of "what happens to families." It is not yet clear what kind of transformation Nicole may be constructing. It is possible that she is invoking a cultural, rather than biological, notion of family, which may be concerned with the consequences of transnational migration on cultural transmission. This vertical transmission along familial lineage may be called into question, but there is not yet adequate evidence to make such a claim.

By uttering "born in your countries," Nicole presupposes that the United States is not the country of the teens. That is, even if the teens were born in the United States, it is still not their country. This resonates with the forever foreigner stereotype of Asian Americans regardless of birthplace. Birthplace, then, both emerges as a meaningful category in the question of "what happens to families" and creates a boundary between a category of "your countries" and a category of "not your countries," namely, the United States. The contrastive connector "or" (line 61) provided in the text contributes to this dichotomy. Already, in such a brief utterance, dichotomous categories emerge that position "America" in opposition to "your countries." Next, positionings along these trajectories become inhabited as teens are recruited to these categories in their reply to Nicole's question.

(8)

```
62   Boi:     I was born in Thailand
63   Nicole:  how about you?
64   Moeun:   I was born here
65   Loc:     I was born here
66   Yem:     I was born in Cambodia but I came here when I
67            was young so I don't know anything much (.) if
68            I came here older I would have experienced
69            more? but I don't even
70   Angie:   Theth?
71   Theth:   born here
```

Within the oppositional categories of "your countries" and "America" laid out by Nicole, Boi, who was born in a refugee camp in Thailand, was born neither in "his country" nor in "America." He doesn't seem to fit within the divisions of nationhood in the emergent schema. The other teens, however, fit neatly into these categories: Moeun, Loc, and Theth were born in "America," not "their countries," and Yem was born in "her country," Cambodia.

Thus far, categories, such as family, birthplace, and current residence, have emerged to interactionally position speech event participants, namely, the teens, within binary categories of nationhood. As the interaction continues, Joe (African American male), an adult audience member, proceeds to fill out this schema introduced by Nicole.

(9)

```
72    Joe:      how much- how much of what you're saying is a
73              cultural value of Cambodia. that girls are
74              protected more are sheltered more and uh
75              expected to (?) and how much of that i::s
76              (1.0) the American society where it's pushing
77              (0.6) um::: (0.8) you guys are out there so
78              you know "hey I gotta play it a certain way"
79              (0.7) a::nd maybe tell your little sister "I
80              don't wanna see you hanging around this (?)
81              but we're- doing this (?)"
82    Loc:      'cau[se
83    Joe:          [how much of it is the socialization of
84              the American rendition of Cambodian values
85              versus (.) Cambodian values
86    Loc:      'cause here in America? you see more bad
87              people than in Cambodia so: if y- if you- if
88              you gonna leave your sister out and stuff?
89              y'know in- in America y- you might be scared
90              for her you mi- no one will protect her. you
91              scared she might get hurt or somethin'? get
92              raped or somethin'? but for a guy? he- he know
93              how to protect himself 'cause he's stronger
94              than a girl an- and your parents- parents
95              this- this- this is what your parents think
96              though. but. I don't really know though <two
97              or three audience members laugh>
```

Added to the spatiotemporal frame laid out by Nicole is the introduction of the idea that each country has a culture (i.e., one country, one culture). Cultural values are distinctively linked to countries: "cultural value of Cambodia" (line 73), "the American society" (line 76), "the socialization of the American rendition of Cambodian values" (lines 83–84), and "Cambodian values" (line 85). The contrastive connectors provided in the text—"and" (line 75) and "versus" (line 85)—continue the structure of oppositional categories within this schema. In addition, notions of "(cultural) value" (lines 73, 84, 85), "society" (line 76), and "socialization" (line 83) emerge and contextualize Nicole's utterance about "what happens to families" within a more explicit discussion involving culture. Thus, the schema is further taking shape as it collectively identifies familial categories—"family" (line 59), "parents" (lines 94, 95) and "sister" (lines 79, 88)—as well as nations—"Cambodia" (lines 66, 73, 84, 85, 87) and "America" (lines 60, 76, 84, 86, 89)—and interactionally positions teens as torn between oppositional cultural values as they move along life trajectories. Next, the distinct division between the teens and their families becomes pivotal in this emergent schema.

(10)

```
98    Nicole:  do you all stick with your families?
99    Moeun:   what do you mean by that? (2.2) [(yeah)
100   Nicole:                                  [are you all
101            (.) involved with your families (.) in their
102            culture
103   Moeun:   yeah
104   Loc:     yea:h
105   Boi:     °yeah°
106   Yem:     °yeah° °h(hh)°
107   Moeun:   °h(hh)° (1.1)
108   Joe:     I- I- I guess- I guess my concern is are you
109            lo:sing your culture
```

Nicole creates a division between the teens and "your families" (line 98), which differentiates culture into two emergent constructs: "your culture" (line 109), that of the teens, and "their culture" (lines 101–102), that of their parents or families. The teens, then, are constructed as having a culture distinct from others, both that of American society and that of their Southeast Asian families. The question "are you losing your culture" (lines 108–109) seems to ask whether or not the teens themselves are holding onto this transmitted essence, namely, their parents' culture.

What has been revealed so far is that certain aspects of culture and identity are being indexed in interactional real time. This indexing builds up oppositional categories inhabitable by the teen panelists. The audience members are positioned as the creators of this schema, and the teens, their parents, sisters, and families—but not the audience members—are positioned as the inhabitors of its categories. These categories involve several distinctions: a distinction between being born in a country and residing in a country, a distinction between people who possess culture and those who lose it, and a distinction between first generation immigrants (the teens' parents) and their 1.5 or second generation children (the teens themselves). Elsewhere the teens may produce these distinctions as well—particularly the generational division, which was explored earlier in this chapter; however, in this particular interaction, the teens are more the inhabitors, as opposed to the creators, of these distinctions.

Identity Politics, Authenticity, and Pluralism

The politics of identity, which legitimizes unity based on ethnic and cultural authenticity (Heller, 1999), is invoked throughout this first schema of culture. Here, culture is emerging as a matter of authenticity, achieved only in "your countries" and either lost or mediated when a group immigrates to a new country and becomes immersed in another culture. This first schema attempts to define culture as a matter of spatiotemporal, authentic, and transmittable values occurring within families. At the same time, it attempts to deconstruct the authenticity of the teen panel, as if the hybrid "American rendition of Cambodian values" is somehow not the authentic "Cambodian values" and may lead the teens to lose their culture as defined. Categories such as these essentialize the Asian American experience and oversimplify complex phenomena, often reducing identity issues to intergenerational tensions or conflicts between nations and cultural value (Lowe, 1996). Furthermore, the concern over the teens losing their culture presupposes that an ideal Asian American be a forever foreigner who retains a distinct culture.

The politics of identity, according to Heller (1999), is shifting from a model rooted in ethnic and linguistic unity to a new model characterized by pluralism and the expansion of capitalism in a globalized economy. As I explore the second emergent schema, a hint of movement in this direction can be detected. In addition to engaging in grassroots video production, which reaches audiences like the one at the school district conference, Moeun reveals another aspiration to be a cultural producer in a capitalist music industry: "I'm tryin' to like put out a CD so um like people know that ... Asian people can do this." This desire for inclusion in a global entertainment market, which is presumed to allow participation by Asian Americans such as Moeun, suggests a movement toward the new model, but not without an investment in the old politics of identity. That is, the old politics of identity, which legitimizes the "Asian" category invoked by Moeun, also fought to establish the right to self-determination for disenfranchised groups (Heller, 1999). But this discourse has also changed the conditions of their existence, namely, by creating hope that inclusiveness is achievable in a more pluralist society. Moeun and others draw on this hope as the discourse continues.

Culture as Emblem of Ethnic Differentiation

The second schema of culture begins where Joe left off: "are you losing your culture." Notice that this utterance is introduced by a member of the audience and thus is one to which the panelists are recruited by having to respond. Amy, an unidentified adult female audience member, enters the discussion as she displays support for Joe's concern (line 110).

(11)

```
108   Joe:    I- I- I guess- I guess my concern is are you
109           lo:sing your culture
110   Amy:    yeah
111   Loc:    not really though [(.) not- not really
112   Joe:                      [naw:: not really because
113           "All Means All" means that- that your culture
114           is valued
115   Loc:    well we try to bring our culture up because
116           er- most people don't really know about our
117           culture so we try and bring it up
118   Amy:    mm hmm (0.7)
119   Loc:    try and let everyone know about it [y'know
```

```
120   Moeun:                                              [we tryin'
121           to put Cambos out there (1.0) y'know (?)
```

After Joe asks "are you losing your culture," a female audience member utters "yeah" (line 110), which may display ratification or sharedness of Joe's question or concern. After Loc replies that he is "not really" losing his culture (line 111), Joe invokes the title of the conference "All Means All" to metapragmatically frame the assertion that "your culture is valued" (lines 113–114).

In the first schema of culture, culture emerged as a construct of internal values transmitted within families, but Loc introduces culture as something to bring out into mainstream society: "we try to bring our culture up" (line 115). Bringing culture up emerges as some form of external display involving people other than their families. Loc indexes "most people" (line 116), who are constructed as unaware of his culture and therefore the reason why his culture needs to be more visible and known to "everyone" (line 119). Moeun ratifies this position and replaces the notion of "our culture" with an ethnic category "Cambos" (line 121). It is from this point on that possessive pronouns completely drop off, suggesting that they are no longer working strictly within the first schema of possessable cultural values; rather, a new schema of ethnic categorization and division is emerging in its place. These categories are made denotationally explicit as the discourse continues.

(12)

```
122   Loc:     'cause most people really know about Japanese
123            Chinese and stuff we tryin'- know abo- tryin'
124            to know about Cambodia and how they [was
125   Moeun:                                      [yeah (.)
126            we want to let people know that y'know like-
127            this- thi- it's not like all Chinese- not
128            Asian people is all Chinese y'know like put
129            like Cambos out there. I wanna- I wanna walk
130            down the street and then like (.) a Black guy
131            be like (.) like- well anybody could say "yo
132            yo he Cambo" y'know?
133   Loc:     yeah not- not like (.) "are you Chinese?"
134            y'know (1.0) not like that (1.4)
135   Moeun:   right now I'm tryin' to do somethin' to put
```

```
136        Cambos out there. <several audience members
137        start talking among themselves> I'm tryin' to
138        like- put out a CD (0.6) so um like people
139        know that y'know Cambos can do this too
140        y'know? like Asian people can do this (9.5)
```

Indexed throughout this excerpt are categories of ethnicity—"Japanese" (line 122), "Chinese" (lines 123, 127, 128, 133), and "Cambodians" (lines 124, 129, 132, 136, 139)—as well as categories of race—"Asian" (lines 128, 140) and "Black" (line 130). This indexical patterning of race and ethnicity emerges to collectively presuppose these categories as meaningful to participants and central to this schema. Teens construct culture as involving not only themselves and their families—"we" (lines 123, 126) and "I" (lines 129, 135, 137)—but also others—"people" (lines 122, 126, 138), "a Black guy" (line 130), and "anybody" (line 131).

"Most people" are constructed as unable to recognize and distinguish among ethnic kinds within the Asian American racial category. This is accomplished, in part, through voicing (Bakhtin, 1935/1981). A voice is an identifiable social position for a character discussed in the denotational text. When voicing characters, speakers also take evaluative stances. For example, when Moeun voices "anybody" in a fictional social world where Cambodian Americans are recognizable, "yo yo he Cambo" (lines 131–132), he is taking an evaluative stance on his own ethnic recognizability in American society, namely, that Cambodian Americans are not recognizable in his current social world. At the same time, through quoted speech, he makes recognizable the type of person he is voicing. This is accomplished by the linguistic utterances "yo" and "Cambo" accompanied by copula ellipsis in "he Cambo." These features may collectively mark African American Vernacular English (AAVE) or an AAVE-influenced urban youth variety spoken by young people like Moeun and Loc who come into contact with Southeast Asian Americans in their neighborhoods and schools. Next, Loc voices the average mainstream American in their current social world, "are you Chinese" (line 133), which supports Moeun's stance that Cambodian Americans are not recognizable. Through patterns of indexical forms, the teens separate themselves from mainstream Americans, who are unable to ethnically recognize Cambodian Americans or distinguish among Asian American ethnic kinds because they draw on the "all Asians are Chinese" and "all Asians look alike" stereotypes.

After Sapna (Indian American female), a school district administrator and
Asian Arts Initiative member, gives names and phone numbers of school district
officials to the audience, Kim (African American female), an adult audience
member, enters the discussion.

(13)

```
141   Kim:     I just had (to feel sorry) about what you just
142            sai:d y'know (having) somebody being able to
143            walk up to you and say "well you're from
144            Cambodia" but um: (0.6) yeah I just think
145            that- I just (?) culture? can't just walk up
146            to somebody and decide where they're from?
147   Moeun:   [no I'm not saying that
148   Loc:     [no:: no
149   Boi:     [no:: no
150   Moeun:   I'm [not saying (?) no at least- at- at least=
151   Kim:         [I'm not just saying you can't (?)
152   Moeun:   =they- I just want them to know that [y'know
153   Loc:                                          [no at
154            least they can know about us y'know (.) but
155            most people you ask them I bet you they- they
156            say they don't know nothin' about Cambodian. I
157            bet you they say they know a whole lot about
158            Chinese, Japanese and stuff but you ask them
159            about Cambodians they be like "who's that
160            what's that"
161   Sapna:   h(hh)mh(hh)m
```

Beginning with an explicit evaluation "I just had (to feel sorry) about what you
just said" (lines 141–142), Kim challenges this emergent schema. She reframes
Moeun's voicing of "them" from "yo yo he Cambo" to "well you're from Cambodia" (lines 143–144) to support her argument that one "can't just walk up to
somebody and decide where they're from" (lines 145–146). Three teens loudly
proclaim "no" (lines 147, 148, 149) in response, and Moeun and Loc defend the
paradigm by making it a matter of "them/people" (lines 152, 154, 155, 156, 157,
158, 159) knowing about "us/Cambodians" (lines 154, 156, 159). Loc illustrates
this by voicing "them" as saying, "who's that what's that" (lines 159–160) when
they are asked about Cambodians. Sapna, who is also Asian American, responds

with laughter (line 161), which may ratify Loc's predication or the comic effect of his voicing.

Speech event participants can be positioned in clearly defined groups of "we/us" and "they/them." The we/us category includes the Asian Americans in the room; that is, the teen panel, Asian Arts Initiative staff and Sapna. The they/them category includes the rest of the audience. They are lumped together with the people who recognize Asian Americans as only Chinese or Japanese, the undesirable current social world constructed by the teens in which Cambodian Americans are rendered unrecognizable.

Multiculturalism, Ethnic Recognizability, and Panethnicity

Multiculturalist discourses of intergroup relations and cultural value are invoked throughout this second schema. Culture becomes more about relationships among racial categories (Asians, Blacks, and Whites, which was invoked later) and ethnic categories (Cambodian, Chinese, and Japanese), rather than about cultural transmission occurring within immigrant families. Unlike the first schema of culture, the second one was constructed primarily by the teens themselves. The teen panel seems to have deconstructed the first schema, asserting that they not only have culture but are also able to redefine it. Culture is not (or at least is more than) a matter of authentic transmittable values; it is indexical of ethnic group membership and differentiation. This reformulation is accompanied by shifts in participation frameworks (Goffman, 1981), with regard to the characters in the denotational text, and the speech event participants in the interactional text.

Throughout this second schema, the teens divide Asian American ethnic groups into categories of ethnic recognizability: On the one hand, there are recognizable Asian ethnic groups, such as Chinese and Japanese Americans, and, on the other hand, there are unrecognizable Asian ethnic groups, such as Cambodian Americans. Mainstream Americans are characterized as drawing on the "all Asians are Chinese" and "all Asians look alike" stereotypes when mistaking the Southeast Asian American teens for more widely circulating East Asian ethnic groups. By producing a music CD in the future and creating videos at the video-making project, the teens actively engage in debunking these stereotypes, attempting to propel the Other Asian into wider circulation to increase their ethnic recognizability. By dividing Asian ethnic groups to argue for increased ethnic recognizability, however, the teens remove themselves from a panethnic Asian American community by focusing on issues of ethnic differentiation between themselves and Chinese and Japanese Americans.

Invoking the motto of liberal multiculturalism, "your culture is valued" (lines 113–114), marks a pivotal moment in this second schema. Prior to this utterance, the audience members were positioning the teens in a paradigm that questioned their authenticity. But following this utterance, an extended discussion of the politics of recognition unfolds. In this second half of the discussion, ethnic and racial categories divide groups into those that are recognized and those that are unrecognized by mainstream Americans. The teens also take up identities that position them as not only holding on to their unrecognized culture but also actively bringing it out into mainstream society. Thus, the teens assert that losing culture is not their problem but the problem of mainstream Americans. That is, before mainstream Americans can value cultural diversity—a claim that Joe makes—they must first recognize it. This critique is a step toward a more critical multiculturalism, which not only confronts the social inequalities that liberal multiculturalism can be accused of ignoring but also demands structural transformation in the name of social justice (cf. McLaren, 1997; Prashad, 2002). The teens, thus, formulate an insightful criticism of liberal multiculturalism: How can their culture be valued if it's not even recognized?

The analysis of this interaction clearly illustrates how macrolevel concepts of culture and ethnicity were not only locatable at the microlevel but also creatively used as performative resources in interaction. Using a circulatory notion of culture, the analysis traces how schemas of intragroup and intergroup relations, cultural value, and ethnic and racial identity were brought forth into circulation, inhabited, and critiqued in this interaction. Rather than being nebulous constructs removed from daily conversation, they were very much experienced by virtue of being indexically invoked under the conditions derived from the interaction itself. The politics of identity was invoked by the audience to position teens as unauthentic recipients of Cambodian culture; the teens challenged liberal multiculturalism by asserting that recognizing cultural difference must precede valuing cultural difference. Thus, broad notions of culture and identity were revealed to have two distinct properties. First, their values were emergent in conversation, interactionally negotiated, and performatively achieved. But also, importantly, they were relational phenomena. That is, their characteristics were not inherent but discernible only in relation to the denotational and interactional details in the conversation.

CONCLUSION

Unlike the previous chapter on the local production of panethnic community, this chapter examined interactional contexts in which the teens deconstructed Asian American panethnicity. Macrolevel concepts of culture, ethnicity, and panethnicity vividly emerged at the level of microlevel interaction, revealing how flexible and multidimensional these concepts are. The teens often constructed mainstream Americans as drawing on the "all Asians are Chinese" and "all Asians look alike" stereotypes and mistaking Southeast Asian Americans for more widely circulating Asian ethnic kinds, namely, Chinese, Japanese, and Korean Americans. The teens were keenly aware of the tensions and affinities between and within particular ethnic groups, revealing the importance of generation as a locally meaningful division of identity that sometimes thwarted their own efforts to construct panethnic community. Most of the teens, however, did not go as far as exhibiting what was locally known as ethnic pride, a form of ethnic superiority and separation that was viewed as the ultimate means of panethnic destruction.

This chapter also explored how the speech chain that circulated images of Southeast Asian American ethnic groups intersected with the speech chain that circulated the value of cultural diversity, resulting in the production of a link between the issue of cultural maintenance and ethnic recognizability. During the conference panel discussion, the teens circumvented the first schema of culture, that of culture as historical transmission, by devising an alternative way of conceptualizing culture as an emblem of ethnic differentiation. In the first schema, the teens were positioned as losing their culture, which presupposed that an ideal Asian American be a forever foreigner who retains a distinct culture. In the second schema, the teens challenged the audience by implicitly asking how their culture could be valued if people could not recognize it. Arguing that they lived in a current world where only East Asian ethnic kinds were recognizable, the teens hoped to live in a future world in which Southeast Asian ethnic groups would be recognized as ethnically distinct. This perspective foregrounded divisions between Asian American ethnic groups at the expense of a unified panethnic formation.

Yet the exploration of panethnicity in these last two chapters revealed how the teens were often able to promote ethnic recognizability and panethnic community simultaneously. Creating videos that portrayed their lives and experiences as members of less recognizable ethnic groups, the teens attempted to defy homogenizing stereotypes of Asian Americans by casting the Other Asian into wider circulation, while invoking homogenizing stereotypes in the local construction of panethnicity. The next and final chapter provides some concluding remarks on the implications of this book as a whole in terms of its methodological approach and its examination of educational and media sites for minority youth.

6

Implications for Minority Youth in Alternative Education and Grassroots Video

Look at the kids in the video. What are they? They're post-Vietnam kids, right? So that's the thing: They're post-Vietnam war kids. They're the immigrant kids and stuff. So you see their experience. You should probably show it to some third generation Chinese kids. You can relate to the universal themes but can't relate to the individual experiences. ... [The videomaking project] helps us to identify ourselves as being like "Hey! We're the Other Asian."

—Sokla, 2002

During one of my routine visits to Philadelphia in the fall of 2004, I attended the "Asian Americans in Hip Hop" event at the Asian Arts Initiative, hoping to see some of the former Southeast Asian American teen participants from the after-school video-making project. Following my 4 years of fieldwork in 1999–2002, I had kept in touch with a handful of teens, but on this particular occasion I was especially hoping to see Moeun (Cambodian Chinese American male), an exceptionally gregarious teenager with whom I had always felt a special connection. Moeun appeared several times throughout the chapters in this book, whether he was claiming that his teachers thought he was "dumb" (chapter 1), effusively deriding "F.O.B.s" (chapter 2), accusing Asian American teenagers of "acting Black" (chapter 3), or discussing how he wanted to "put Cambos out there" so that people would realize that not all Asian Americans were Chinese (chapter 5).

After the 3rd year of the after-school video-making project ended in 2001, Moeun rarely visited the Asian Arts Initiative. Yet staff members and former teen participants of the video-making project assured me that he would be attending the hip hop event. This did not entirely surprise me given that Moeun participated in several aspects of hip hop culture: as a break dancer, DJ, graffiti artist, rapper, and R&B singer and songwriter. Throughout the years, the video-making project and the Asian Arts Initiative routinely provided opportunities for Moeun to explore and hone his wide range of interests and talents: For example, he designed and provided artwork for some publicity materials, he sang R&B music at various talent showcases, he DJ-ed at a few events, and he displayed his break dancing, rapping, and graffiti art skills in the 1999 teen-created video *American Sroksrei*, in which he portrayed a reformed gang member. Moeun also participated in programs that the Asian Arts Initiative designed directly in response to his and other teens' interests, such as a hip hop dance workshop in the summer of 1999 and a hip hop series in the fall of 2000. But among all of his diverse pursuits, Moeun most frequently expressed his determination to write, record, and release an R&B record and prove that Cambodian Americans could participate in the music industry.[1] This was his dream ever since I first met him in 1999 when he was 15 years old.

As I walked into the familiar teal blue room for the hip hop event at the Asian Arts Initiative, I easily spotted Moeun from across the room. Though I hadn't seen him in nearly 3 years, at age 20 his physical appearance had changed little: Although his frame had slightly broadened, he wore his usual baseball hat and loose clothing. He greeted me with a wide smile and warm hug and introduced me to his girlfriend. As we exchanged various details about our lives, Moeun enthusiastically reported that he was still actively pursuing his R&B singing and songwriting and that he and his friend planned to release their CD in June 2005. He also told me that he had never gone back to high school to graduate after dropping out, that he worked for a while at a car garage and lot but was currently unemployed, and that he still lived with his parents in South Philadelphia, lending an occasional hand at the small corner store his family owned. Though Moeun seemed to enjoy dabbling in film and acting when he participated in the video-making project, as of 2004 he was not pursuing these areas further but holding steadfastly to his longtime dream of releasing an R&B record.

---

[1]See chapter 5 for a transcript of Moeun discussing this in more detail.

Also as of 2004, Lena (Cambodian Chinese Vietnamese American female) at age 19 was majoring in film and media arts at her university, the same university from which Sokla (Cambodian American male) graduated with the same major in the spring of 2004. Introduced to the fundamentals of film production at the Asian Arts Initiative, both Lena and Sokla proclaimed that they were deeply inspired by the after-school video-making project to pursue careers in media arts. Lena told me at the hip hop event, however, that she recently changed her major to electrical engineering. Yet by majoring in engineering, Lena explained that she was actually pursuing—not abandoning—her dream of having a film career. After graduating from the 5-year program in the spring of 2007, Lena was hoping to obtain a computer graphics position at an animation studio, where she could work in the film industry by combining her artistic and technical skills. Even outside of school, Lena remained passionately involved in media arts, whether she was hired by or volunteering for organizations for various video making or film marketing work. For example, in the summer of 2004, Lena was the film distributor for the Asian Arts Initiative through the work-study program offered by her university. Her duties included researching film festivals and competitions and submitting videos created by participants in the Asian Arts Initiative video programs.[2] She also used her video skills to assist other organizations, such as a local Asian American organization through which she received a college scholarship in 2002. Lena created a publicity video about the organization for their annual benefit banquet in 2003.

Despite the different life paths that Moeun and Lena were traveling—high school dropout versus college student, unemployed versus work-study student, R&B singer versus videographer—the after-school video-making project played a similarly vital role in positively shaping their lives and those of many other Southeast Asian American teenagers. The after-school project certainly exposed teens most obviously to the technical and creative aspects of film production—including scriptwriting, lighting, acting, and editing—but perhaps more important it offered youth an open yet structured space to explore and express their identities. As Sokla articulated in the quote that opens this chapter, video making provided the teens a means to identify themselves as post-1975 Cambodian, Lao, and Vietnamese immigrants: the Other Asian. Through the

---

[2]Although the after-school video-making project that I researched ended in 2002 after its 4-year run, the Asian Arts Initiative continued to offer other various video-making programs for both youth and adults.

video-making project, the Southeast Asian American teens had access to a rare program designed specifically for them, where they could both reflect on their unique experiences as Southeast Asian refugee minority youth growing up in urban Philadelphia and artistically create media representations based on their lives for public consumption.

In this concluding chapter, I discuss broader implications of this book. I first underscore the advantages of the methodological approach used in this study to examine how individuals make use of broad macrolevel concepts in situated discursive practice. This chapter also addresses the benefits and challenges of alternative educational settings and grassroots video-making programs for minority youth. I suggest that the findings regarding this particular group of Asian American teenagers add to the understanding of the experiences and perspectives of other linguistic, racial, and immigrant minorities in other parts of the United States and in other educational and media sites.

LANGUAGE, IDENTITY, AND STEREOTYPE

An overarching finding of this book is that seemingly broad and rigid categories are actually quite flexible and multidimensional in local social practice. Consider the term "Asian American." In chapters 1 and 4, Sokla either rejected or accepted being labeled Asian American depending on various situational factors. Whereas at times he emphasized his identity as the Other Asian as separate from Asian American, at other times he foregrounded his participation in Asian American social and political movements. Sokla illustrated the reciprocal relationship between macrolevel and microlevel social orders by, on the one hand, drawing on broad categories in the local management of his identity and, on the other hand, transforming these categories through his creative use of them.

This book examined this macro-micro interplay by exploring the intersection of language, identity, and stereotype. Specifically, the chapters closely analyzed how it was possible for individuals to interactionally construct a positive sense of who they were with widely circulating stereotypes. Chapters 2 and 3, for example, considered how the teens locally managed the stereotypes of Asian Americans as forever foreigners and problem minorities in broad U.S. racial discourses. I examined how the teens routinely invoked stereotypes about Asian newcomers and African Americans largely through ideological links created between these person categories and the following linguistic categories: Mock Asian and slang, respectively. The teens drew on these discursive resources in various ways, positioning themselves close to or away from these broad categories of persons and speech in the local performance of their identities. In addition, concepts such as race and ethnicity, which are often popularly understood as fixed and given categories, emerged with variable elasticity depending on how stereotypes were used as interactional resources. Chapters 4 and 5 illustrated how the wide-scale social organizing principle of panethnicity was locally and flexibly assembled or dismantled depending on the conversational contexts within which stereotypes were used. The methodological approach in this book, which combined ethnography with the close analysis of discourse, proved critical in examining how such macrolevel and microlevel relationships are both inextricably intertwined and mutually informing.

By closely examining interaction over extended periods of time, this book revealed how stereotypes—widespread typifications linking attributes to entities—are much more complex than is commonly perceived. Rather than being mere homogenizing representations applied oppressively to others, stereotypes can be flexibly applied to the self in the creative construction of identity. In chapter 4, for example, by invoking and inhabiting the Asian martial arts stereotype, Van (Vietnamese American female) was able to achieve a local interactional goal: add emphasis to her playful, and perhaps flirtatious, threat to a male teenager. Although invoking this stereotype was permissible in this particular interaction among Asian Americans, the teens largely resented the use of this stereotype by non-Asian Americans. Thus audience as well as several other contextual factors, such as topic of conversation and interactional goals, proved to matter greatly in the use and interpretation of a given stereotype. Moreover, some teens applied African American stereotypes to themselves to construct an urban minority youth identity (chapter 3) or used Asian American stereotypes to lay claim to a separate Other Asian identity (chapter 5). Stereotypes also became interactional resources for crossing in and out of particular identities. For instance, in chapter 2 the teens accessed indexical resources to sometimes identify with the Asian newcomer stereotype and sometimes distance themselves far from it, often within the same utterance. Throughout each of these chapters, stereotypes frequently emerged not as restrictive obstructions to identity formation but as complex interactional resources in the performance of multiple and fluid identities.

ALTERNATIVE EDUCATION

Much research has documented the inadequacies of mainstream education in serving Asian Americans and other racial, immigrant, and linguistic minorities. For instance, several studies examine the prevalence of the honorary White or model minority myth in schools and the blanket application of this stereotype onto young Asian Americans (e.g., S. Lee, 1996). Yet contrary to the image of Asian American youth as "whiz kids," as depicted on the cover of *Time* in August 1987, many struggle at school and with poverty and racism. Fortunately, this image of Asian American success has been challenged by much research that uncovers the diverse and complex experiences of young Asian Americans (e.g., Hune & Chan, 2000; Nakanishi & Hirano-Nakanishi, 1983; Trueba et al., 1993). In Stacey Lee's (1996) ethnography, for example, many high school teachers and administrators buy into the model minority stereotype, despite the wide range of academic achievement and attitudes toward schooling among their Asian American students. She argues that the model minority stereotype thus functions to silence both the voices of low-achieving students and the complexity of high-achieving students' experiences.

The model minority stereotype also silences the reality of anti-Asian sentiment and racial harassment in schools, particularly considering the recent dramatic escalation of hate crimes at countless primary and secondary schools and college campuses (e.g., Kagiwada, 1989; Kiang & Kaplan, 1994; Semons, 1991). Kiang, Nguyen, and Sheehan (1995), for example, described the profile of anti-Asian hostility at one urban high school. They found that despite numerous complaints of various forms of abuse experienced by Asian American students, school officials refused to admit that racism was a problem. In part, the school wanted to uphold its image as an elite institution with no racial tensions. And, in part, the denial that Asian Americans could experience discrimination is a result of both the exclusion and invisibility of Asian Americans in discussions of race and the model minority stereotype that perpetuates the erroneous image that all Asian Americans succeed in schools and integrate seamlessly into American society. Moreover, anti-Asian violence has only increased in and out of schools after the events of September 11, 2001, and in the current anti-immigration political climate (e.g., Klein, 2005), both of which draw on the stereotype that all "Orientals" are alike (e.g., South Asian Sikhs mistaken for

Middle Easterners) and foreign (e.g., Asian Americans perceived as immigrants that do not belong in the United States).

Because schools can fail to provide a space that is both beneficial and safe for Asian Americans and other minority groups, many young people are often left searching for these qualities in other places, such as gangs and alternative education. The lure of gangs or other types of street culture was a reality for many of the Southeast Asian American teenagers at the video-making project. In this sense, the teens were not unlike Asian American youth in other parts of the United States: for example, Vietnamese American youth who organize in the form of gangs in Los Angeles (Vigil & Yun, 1990); Chinese American youth who constitute more than half of the members of Chinatown gangs in New York City (Chin, 1996); and several immigrant Cambodian, Laotian, and Korean American youth who join gangs in urban areas as well (Badey, 1988; Knox, 1992).[3] Often striving to incorporate the sense of belonging, safety, and opportunity that gangs provide, alternative educational settings aspire to succeed where schools fail (Irby & McLaughlin, 1990). Over the past decade, several educational researchers have increasingly shifted their attention to such after-school programs and informal educational sites (e.g., Eccles & Gootman, 2002; Hull & Schultz, 2002; Weis & Fine, 2000). In their 5-year study of 60 youth organizations, for example, Heath and McLaughlin (1993) found that "most of the young who come to these organizations, in fact, regard school as a place that has rejected and labeled them by *what they are not* rather than by *what they are*" (p. 4). Centered around a particular activity or educational goal, many after-school programs allow youth to form safe group affiliations where their voices and local knowledge are valued and incorporated into the institution to reorganize new structures of participation and learning (Heath, 1999a).

A significant finding of this book is that the after-school video-making project provided underserved Southeast Asian American teenagers with a vital site for exploring and expressing their identities. This finding has implications not only for Asian American youth but for other racial, immigrant, and linguistic minorities whose needs are also often overlooked in schools. The overall success of the video-making project was achieved through a constellation of methods: for example, supplying a safe space, fostering a sense of community, promoting

---

[3]The reality of Asian American gang participation has partly disrupted the model minority myth, but only by replacing it with another stereotype: the problem minority. See chapter 1 for a further discussion of the emergence of the problem minority stereotype.

open dialogue, valuing the local knowledge of youth and integrating it into the fabric of the program, working *with* not *for* young people through youth–practitioner collaboration, encouraging youth to think and act critically, teaching youth technical and creative skills, working toward an attainable and tangible end product, exposing youth to different career paths, and creating additional programs in response to youth interests. By structuring the video-making project around the exploration of issues youth themselves identified as important, the Southeast Asian American teenagers were able to broach, explore, discuss, and analyze sensitive topics and social issues that had direct relevance to their lives, such as gangs, drug use, sexuality, and interracial, interethnic, and intergenerational tensions, issues that are likely either not addressed in schools or addressed in a didactic manner. Adult staff strived to listen to youth compassionately yet critically and without judgment. This helped create an overall atmosphere of understanding, acceptance, and comfort, where youth identities were explored, not silenced. The after-school video-making project provided valuable opportunities for young people, many of whom were struggling in schools and on the streets, to explore other styles of learning, other ways of being, and other paths outside of formal schooling.

Beyond these core aspects of the after-school video-making project that are also shared by many other alternative educational settings documented in the research literature, I suggest another perhaps less common factor that significantly aided in its success: sharedness of participant backgrounds. Similarity of racial and ethnic background, not only between youth and adults but also among youth, seemed to prove critical to the open dialogue that was often achieved among participants and practitioners. This program, created by a group of enthusiastic and innovative Asian American medical students and sustained for 4 years by a remarkable and dedicated Asian American community organization, was built on a strong commitment to Asian American youth, who were often failed by the types of formal learning environments that schools provide. This racial homogeneity, which was rarely found elsewhere in the teens' lives (particularly in their schools), may have been critical in opening up channels of communication based on a shared racial identity. This book, however, revealed that sharedness of racial identity, as well as ethnic, linguistic, class, and other types of identity, was an achieved social product rather than a natural given category (cf. Rymes, 1996). For example, the teens sometimes highlighted linguistic differences along Asian American generational lines, through constructing Asian newcomer speech as spoken primarily by adults (chapter 2) or constructing African American slang as spoken primarily by youth (chapter 3). They also highlighted distinctions between different Asian ethnic groups, such as Cambodian and Vietnamese (chapter 5). Because allowing youth to explore their unique identities as the Other Asian was an integral component of the video-making project, for the most part it seemed to matter little that most of the adults were not of Southeast Asian descent. However, it seemed important that the adults were at least Asian American, giving the teens the opportunity to explore their identities within a rare institution that fostered a sense of a panethnic community (chapter 4).

I do not wish to imply, however, that the after-school video-making project was always successful in achieving its program goals and creating an ideal atmosphere. As do several other alternative educational sites, the video-making project constantly struggled with how to work with youth without relying on didactic pedagogical styles and without reproducing a formal educational space. Openly and critically addressing these struggles was ongoing at the video-making project and, I believe, indicative of the concern for and devotion to providing the best possible educational space for Asian American youth.

GRASSROOTS VIDEO MAKING

Although after-school projects often center around a particular activity or instructional goal, such as sports (e.g., Petitpas & Champagne, 2000), health (e.g., Shepperson, 1985), or compensatory education (e.g., Hamovitch, 1997), much recent scholarly attention has been centered on arts programs (e.g., Ball & Heath, 1993; Gullotta & Plant, 2000; Heath, 1999a, 1999b; Heath & Smyth, 1999). Though art was often used in social change efforts during the ethnic pride movements in the 1960s and 1970s, it is still commonly seen as irrelevant or extravagant in poor urban areas plagued by adversity (Ball & Heath, 1993). Yet youth in these programs often use "art to express current dimensions of their lives: their battles with drugs and gangs and their efforts to cope with ways to announce some achievement and identity for themselves" (Ball & Heath, 1993, pp. 71–72). Broadened understanding of its potential role in community building has led youth organizations to look increasingly to the arts as a way to build discipline, commitment, confidence, leadership skills, and a sense of group solidarity and connectedness (Gullotta & Plant, 2000; Heath, 1999a, 1999b). Arts programs also foster critical thinking skills by allowing youth to explore and express personal and collective stories that create alternative ways of viewing and understanding the world.

The alternative educational site in this book was an arts program developed partly in response to mass media representations of Asian Americans. Public sphere circulation of group representations plays a powerful role in how groups are understood and understand themselves. Habermas's (1989) claim that the public sphere is a restricted, rather than participatory, space is easily applicable to the character of mass media. That is, to participate in media production, one has to have access to the means by which it is produced. Hebdige (1993) writes:

> [A]ccess to the means by which ideas are disseminated in our society (i.e. principally the mass media) is *not* the same for all classes. Some groups have more say, more opportunity to make the rules, to organize meaning, while others are less favourably placed, have less power to produce and impose their definitions of the world on the world. (p. 365)

Yet in the past several decades, the development of affordable film and video technologies has caused a degree of decentralization of media control. Growing numbers of people need not rely on the backing of large film studios to produce movies that can potentially reach wide audiences; instead, people can seek support through media advocacy groups and small grassroots studios in the production, marketing, and distribution of independent film. For example, *Super Size Me* (Spurlock, 2004a), a feature-length documentary about a man who for 1 month ate only fast food from McDonald's, the multibillion dollar global food-service empire, was made on a mere $75,000 budget. Yet this film had a wide impact with a broad commercial release, an Academy Award nomination, and influence over the McDonald's Corporation to end its super-sizing feature on its menu (Spurlock, 2004b). Certainly, the majority of independently produced films are rarely met with such parallel success, but *Super Size Me* nonetheless illustrates the increasing potential impact of grassroots modes of art and activism.

Much Asian American grassroots media has also been used to critically address social issues. In particular, Asian American–produced films and videos are frequently used to challenge political injustices and homogenizing stereotypes affecting Asian Americans (Fung, 1994; Xing, 1998). Beginning with *Chan is*

Missing (Wang, 1982)—one of the first feature-length theatrical releases with an all-Asian American cast and crew—Asian American films often produce representations that subvert those widely circulating in mainstream media, namely, the stereotypes of the forever foreigner and model minority (Xing, 1998). Two examples of independently-produced films that explicitly address social injustices are *All Orientals Look the Same* (1985) by Valerie Soe and *Who Killed Vincent Chin?* (1989) by Christine Choy and Renee Tajima. The former is a visual procession of different Asian faces while the title phrase repeats continuously. This simple juxtaposition addresses an issue that emerged with great significance in chapter 5: that Asian Americans are perceived as indistinguishable from one another. *Who Killed Vincent Chin?* demonstrates a consequence of this very stereotype: Vincent Chin, a Chinese American, was brutally killed in Detroit in 1982 by White, unemployed autoworkers who thought he was Japanese. Reportedly motivated by their anger over the booming Japanese automobile industry in the 1980s, these men were subsequently acquitted and spent not a single day in jail. The film probes this case further and ultimately asks if justice was served.

The after-school video-making project in this study was also engaged in the production of Asian American grassroots media. Each of the four teen-created videos—*American Sroksrei* (1999), *249* (2000), *Ba. Bay. Three.* (2001), and *These Are the Days* (2002)—tackles pressing social issues from the youth perspective. For example, *American Sroksrei* is largely about gangs, violence, and hip hop; *249* primarily addresses intergenerational issues and gender roles in immigrant families; *Ba. Bay. Three.* deals mainly with interethnic prejudice among Southeast Asian Americans; and *These Are the Days* discusses the role peer pressure plays in romantic relationships. For the most part, the videos focus on how these issues specifically concern Asian American communities. But more generally, the videos touch on "universal themes," to quote Sokla at the beginning of this chapter, that have relevance to the lives of other urban, minority, or immigrant youth throughout the United States. Although the videos have not enjoyed a wide commercial release, they have been shown at numerous schools, universities, community organizations, museums, conferences, small movie theaters, and film festivals in Philadelphia, New York City, and Washington, DC.

An overarching finding of this book is that grassroots video making can be an exceptionally effective type of alternative arts program for all types of youth, particularly racial, immigrant, and linguistic minority youth whose lives are of-ten problematically represented in mainstream media. First, the after-school video-making project integrated new technologies into its programming, which proved to be extremely appealing to the teen participants. The teens generally enjoyed not only learning about new technologies but also applying and building on the technological skills that they already had (because of their often vast knowledge of computers, cell phones, pagers, and other technological devices). The operation of digital video cameras and digital video editing software, as well as other film technologies, such as lighting and sound equipment, was often swiftly learned by the teen participants—often at a faster pace than the adult volunteers—which served to enhance their sense of competence and self-esteem. Second, the sheer awe of making a film motivated most of the teenagers to think and act critically about the kinds of media representations they were responding to and the kinds of media representations they wanted to create. The teens were given a rare opportunity to be responsible for creating their own Asian American film representations, which forced the teens to confront issues regarding media, representation, and stereotype in a very real and concrete way. These critical thinking skills were often developed as the teens negotiated various representa-tions, from speech styles of the characters, such as nonnative English (chapter 2) and slang (chapter 3), to professions of the characters, such as storeowner (chapter 4). Third, through specialized skills development in film technologies, scriptwriting, and acting, the craft of video making exposed the teens to several possible career paths. Some teens, such as Lena and Sokla, were directly in-spired to pursue film careers, and other teens, such as Moeun, were influenced to pursue similar artistic dreams involving different modes of expression, namely, singing and songwriting. Finally, the video-making project was designed so that the teens were working toward the goal of a finished product. Because each project year culminated in a video, the teens left the after-school program with a tangible object that represented the proud result of a collaborative effort.

Because media transcends both temporal and spatial boundaries, the poten-tial is there for the videos created through the after-school video-making project to reach wide audiences across countless locations. Unfortunately, however, on a national—let alone global—scale, there is little demand for the teen-created videos or for, more broadly, films produced by or featuring Asian Americans. Though the years between the occasional Asian American film success are be-coming fewer—*Flower Drum Song* (Koster, 1961), *Joy Luck Club* (Wang,

1993), *Better Luck Tomorrow* (Lin, 2002), and *Harold and Kumar Go to White Castle* (Leiner, 2004)—not too much has changed with regard to the paucity of Asian American representations controlled by Asian Americans. Through grassroots efforts, however, the Southeast Asian American teenagers were part of a larger movement of minority filmmakers and producers who document the lives of those seldom seen or heard.

By paying attention to the particular experiences and perspectives of the Southeast Asian American teenagers in this book, I hope to have revealed the complexity and importance of their lives, not only by examining how stereotypes were flexibly used in the linguistic construction of youth identities but also by exploring how through alternative education and grassroots video making, young people—particularly minority youth—have much to offer and gain through engaging in unique and valuable educational and media sites, like the one offered by the after-school video-making project.

References

Agha, A. (1998). Stereotypes and registers of honorific language. *Language in Society, 27*, 151–193.

Agha, A. (2003). The social life of cultural value. *Language and Communication, 23*(3), 231–273.

Badey, J. (1988). *Dragons and tigers.* Loomis, CA: Palmer.

Bailey, B. (2002). *Language, race, and negotiation of identity: A study of Dominican Americans.* New York: LFB Scholarly Publishing.

Bakhtin, M. (1981). *The dialogic imagination.* Austin: University of Texas. (Original work published 1935)

Bakhtin, M. (1984). *Problems with Dostoevsky's poetics.* Minneapolis: University of Minnesota Press. (Original work published 1929)

Ball, A., & Heath, S. B. (1993). Dances of identity: Finding an ethnic self in the arts. In S. B. Heath & M. W. McLaughlin (Eds.), *Identity and inner-city youth: Beyond ethnicity and gender* (pp. 69–93). New York: Teachers College Press.

Bancroft, T. & Cook, B. (Directors). (1998). *Mulan* [Motion picture]. Burbank, CA: Walt Disney Pictures.

Barnes, J. S., & Bennett, C. E. (2002). *The Asian population: 2000* (Census 2000 Brief, C2KBR/01-16). Washington, DC: U.S. Census Bureau.

Barth, F. (Ed.). (1969). *Ethnic groups and boundaries: The social organization of culture difference.* Boston: Little, Brown.

Baugh, J. (1983). *Black street speech: Its history, structure and survival.* Austin: University of Texas Press.

Baugh, J. (1999). *Out of the mouths of slaves: African American language and educational malpractice.* Austin: University of Texas Press.

Baugh, J. (2000). *Beyond Ebonics: Linguistic pride and racial prejudice.* New York: Oxford University Press.

Bauman, R., & Briggs, C. (1990). Poetics and performance as critical perspectives on language and social life. *Annual Review of Anthropology, 19*, 59–88.

Beebe, L. (1985). Input: Choosing the right stuff. In S. Grass & C. Madden (Eds.), *Input in second language acquisition* (pp. 404–414). Rowley, MA: Newbury House.

Bell, A. (1984). Language style as audience design. *Language in Society, 13*(2), 145–204.

Benveniste, E. (1971). *Problems in general linguistics.* Coral Gables, FL: University of Miami Press. (Original work published 1954)

Bourdieu, P. (1991). *Language and symbolic power*. Cambridge, MA: Harvard University Press.

Bucholtz, M. (1997). *Borrowed blackness: African American vernacular English and European American youth identities*. Unpublished doctoral dissertation, University of California, Berkeley.

Bucholtz, M. (1999). You da man: Narrating the racial other in the production of white masculinity. *Journal of Sociolinguistics, 3*(4), 443–460.

Bucholtz, M. (2004). Styles and stereotypes: The linguistic negotiation of identity among Laotian American youth. *Pragmatics, 14*(2/3), 127–148.

Bucholtz, M. (in press). Word up: Social meanings of slang in California youth culture. In J. Goodman & L. Monaghan (Eds.), *Interpersonal communication: An ethnographic approach*. Malden, MA: Blackwell.

Bucholtz, M., & Hall, K. (2003). Language and identity. In A. Duranti (Ed.), *A companion to linguistic anthropology* (pp. 369–394). Malden, MA: Blackwell.

Burks, A. (1948). Icon, index, and symbol. *Philosophy and Phenomenological Research, 9*, 673–689.

Chapman, R. L. (Ed.). (1986). *New dictionary of American slang*. New York: Harper & Row.

Chin, K. (1996). *Chinatown gangs: Extortion, enterprise, and ethnicity*. Oxford, UK: Oxford University Press.

Choy, C., & Tajima, R. (Directors). (1989). *Who killed Vincent Chin?* [Video]. San Francisco, CA: Center for Asian American Media.

Chun, E. (2001). The construction of white, black, and Korean American identities through African American vernacular English. *Journal of Linguistic Anthropology, 11*(1), 52–64.

Chun, E. (2004). Ideologies of legitimate mockery: Margaret Cho's revoicings of Mock Asian. *Pragmatics, 14*(2/3), 236–289.

Coupland, N. (1985). "Hark, hark, the lark": Social motivations for phonological style-shifting. *Language and Communication, 5*(3), 153–172.

Coupland, N. (2001). Dialect stylization in radio talk. *Language in Society, 30*, 345–375.

Cutler, C. A. (1999). Yorkville crossing: White teens, hip hop and African American English. *Journal of Sociolinguistics, 3*(4), 428–442.

Duranti, A. (1997). *Linguistic anthropology*. Cambridge, UK: Cambridge University Press.

De Mille, C. B. (Director). (1915). *The cheat* [Motion picture]. Hollywood, CA: Jesse L. Lasky Feature Play Company.

Eble, C. (1996). *Slang and sociability: In-group language among college students*. Chapel Hill: University of North Carolina Press.

Eble, C. (2004). Slang. In E. Finegan & J. R. Rickford (Eds.), *Language in the USA: Themes for the twenty-first century* (pp. 375–386). Cambridge, UK: Cambridge University Press.

Eccles, J., & Gootman, J. (Eds.). (2002). *Community programs to promote youth development*. Washington, DC: National Academy Press.

Eckert, P. (2000). *Linguistic variation as social practice: The linguistic construction of identity in Belten High*. Oxford, UK: Blackwell.

Eckert, P., & Rickford, J. R. (2001). *Style and sociolinguistic variation*. Cambridge, UK: Cambridge University Press.

Eisenstein, M. (1982). A study of social variation in adult second language acquisition. *Language Learning, 32*, 367–391.

Ellis, R. (1994). *The study of second language acquisition*. Oxford, UK: Oxford University Press.

Espiritu, Y. L. (1992). *Asian American panethnicity: Bridging institutions and identities*. Philadelphia: Temple University Press.

Fine, M. (1991). *Framing dropouts: Notes on the politics of an urban high school*. Albany: State University of New York Press.

Foley, D. E. (1996). The silent Indian as a cultural production. In B. A. Levinson, D. E. Foley, & D. C. Holland (Eds.), *The cultural production of the educated person: Critical ethnographies of schooling and local practice* (pp. 79–91). Albany: State University of New York Press.

Fong, T. (1998). Reflections on teaching about Asian American communities. In L. Hirabayashi (Ed.), *Teaching Asian America: Diversity and the problem of community* (pp. 143–150). Lanham, MD: Rowman & Littlefield.

Fought, C. (2003). *Chicano English in context*. New York: Palgrave MacMillan.

Fung, R. (1994). Seeing yellow: Asian identities in film and video. In K. Aguilar-San Juan (Ed.), *The state of Asian America: Activism and resistance in the 1990s* (pp. 161–172). Boston: South End Press.

Gal, S. (1989). Language and political economy. *Annual Review of Anthropology, 18*, 345–367.

Gal, S. (1998). Multiplicity and contention among language ideologies. In B. Schieffelin, K. Woolard, & P. Kroskrity (Eds.), *Language ideologies: Practice and theory* (pp. 317–332). New York: Oxford University Press.

Gergen, K., & Kaye, J. (1992). Beyond narrative in the negotiation of therapeutic meaning. In S. McNamee & K. Gergen (Eds.), *Therapy as social construction* (pp. 166–185). London: Sage.

Gibson, M. (1988). *Accommodation without assimilation: Sikh immigrants in an American high school*. Ithaca, NY: Cornell University Press.

Gilbert, G. (1951). Stereotype persistence and change among college students. *Journal of Abnormal and Social Psychology, 46*, 245–254.

Giles, H., Taylor, D. M., & Bourhis, R. Y. (1973). Towards a theory of interpersonal accommodation through speech: Some Canadian data. *Language in Society, 2*, 177–192.

Goffman, E. (1974). *Frame analysis: An essay on the organization of experience.* New York: Harper & Row.

Goffman, E. (1981). *Forms of talk.* Philadelphia: University of Pennsylvania Press.

Goldstein, L. (1987). Standard English: The only target for nonnative speakers of English? *TESOL Quarterly, 21*(3), 417–436.

Goodwin, C. (1981). *Conversational organization.* New York: Academic Press.

Goodwin, C., & Goodwin, M. (1992). Assessments and the construction of context. In A. Duranti & C. Goodwin (Eds.), *Rethinking context: Language as an interactive phenomenon* (pp. 147–189). Cambridge, UK: Cambridge University Press.

Goodwin, M. (1990). *He-said she-said: Talk as social organization among black children.* Indianapolis: Indiana University Press.

Goodwin, M. (1999). Constructing opposition within girls' games. In M. Bucholtz, A. Liang, & L. Sutton (Eds.), *Reinventing identities: The gendered self in discourse* (pp. 388–409). New York: Oxford University Press.

Green, L. (2004). African American English. In E. Finegan & J. R. Rickford (Eds.), *Language in the USA: Themes for the twenty-first century* (pp. 76–91). Cambridge, UK: Cambridge University Press.

Griffith, D. W. (Director). (1919). *Broken blossoms* [Motion picture]. Hollywood, CA: Paramount Pictures.

Gullotta, C., & Plant, R. (2000). Promoting social competence through the arts. In S. Danish & T. Gullotta (Eds.), *Developing competent youth and strong communities through after-school programming* (pp. 173–182). Washington, DC: Child Welfare League of America Press.

Habermas, J. (1989). *The structural formation of the public sphere.* Cambridge, MA: MIT Press.

Hagedorn, J. (1994). Asian American women in film: No joy, no luck. *Ms. Magazine, 4*(4), 74–79.

Hall, S. (1988). New ethnicities. *ICA Documents, 7,* 27–31.

Hall, S. (1990). Cultural identity and diaspora. In J. Rutherford (Ed.), *Identity: Community, culture, difference* (pp. 222–237). London: Lawrence and Wishart.

Hall, S. (1996) Introduction: Who needs "identity"? In S. Hall & P. du Gay (Eds.), *Questions of cultural identity* (pp. 1–17). London: Sage.

Halliday, M. A. K. (1976). Anti-languages. *American Anthropologist, 78,* 570–583.

Hamamoto, D. (1994). *Monitored peril: Asian Americans and the politics of TV representation.* Minneapolis: University of Minnesota Press.

Hamovitch, B. (1997). *Staying after school: At-risk students in a compensatory education program.* Westport, CT: Praeger.

Hanna, D. B. (1997). Do I sound "Asian" to you? Linguistic markers of Asian American identity. In C. Boberg, M. Meyerhoff, & S. Strassel (Eds.), *University of Pennsylvania Working Papers in Linguistics, 4*(2), 141–153.

Hatala, E. (1976). *Environmental effects on white students in black schools.* Unpublished master's thesis, University of Pennsylvania, Philadelphia.

He, A. (2001). The language of ambiguity: Practices in Chinese heritage language classes. *Discourse Studies, 3*(1), 75–96.

Heath, S. B. (1983). *Ways with words: Language, life, and work in communities and classrooms.* Cambridge, UK: Cambridge University Press.

Heath, S. B. (1999a). Imaginative actuality: Learning through the arts during the non-school hours. In E. Fiske (Ed.), *Champions of change: The impact of the arts on learning* (pp. 20-34).Washington, DC: Arts Education Partnership and President's Committee on the Arts and the Humanities.

Heath. S. B. (1999b). Living the arts through language + learning: A report on community-based youth organizations. *Monographs, 2*(7), 20–34.

Heath, S. B., & McLaughlin, M. W. (1993). Building identities for inner-city youth. In S. B. Heath & M. W. McLaughlin (Eds.), *Identity and inner-city youth: Beyond ethnicity and gender* (pp. 1–12). New York: Teachers College Press.

Heath, S. B., & Smyth, L. (Directors). (1999). *ArtShow: Youth and community development* [Video]. Washington, DC: Partners for Livable Communities.

Hebdige, D. (1993). From culture to hegemony. In S. During (Ed.), *The cultural studies reader* (pp. 357–367). London: Routledge.

Heller, M. (1999). *Linguistic minorities and modernity: A sociolinguistic ethnography.* New York: Longman.

Hewitt, R. (1982). White adolescent creole users and the politics of friendship. *Journal of Multilingual and Multicultural Development, 3*(3), 217–232.

Hewitt, R. (1986). *White talk, black talk: Inter-racial friendship and communication amongst adolescents.* Cambridge, UK: Cambridge University Press.

Hill, J. (1995). Mock Spanish: A site for the indexical reproduction of racism in American English. *Language and Culture Online Symposium, 2.*

Hughes, J. (Director). (1984). *Sixteen candles* [Motion picture]. Universal City, CA: Universal Pictures.

Hull, G., & Schultz, K. (Eds.). (2002). *School's out! Bridging out-of-school literacies with classroom practice.* New York: Teachers College Press.

Hune, S., & Chan, K. (1999). Educating Asian Pacific Americans: Struggles and progress. In T. Fong & L. Shinagawa (Eds.), *Asian Americans: Experiences and perspectives* (pp. 141–168). Upper Saddle River, NJ: Prentice Hall.

Hymes, D. (1974). *Foundations in sociolinguistics: An ethnographic approach.* Philadelphia: University of Pennsylvania Press.

Irby, M., & McLaughlin, M. W. (1990). When is a gang not a gang? When it's a tumbling team. *Future Choices, 2,* 31–41.

Irvine, J. (1989). When talk isn't cheap: Language and political economy. *American Ethnologist, 16,* 248–267.

Irvine, J. (2001). Style as distinctiveness: The culture and ideology of linguistic differentiation. In P. Eckert & J. R. Rickford (Eds.), *Style and sociolinguistic variation* (pp. 21–43). Cambridge, UK: Cambridge University Press.

Jagose, A. (1997). *Queer theory: An introduction.* New York: New York University Press.

Jakobson, R. (1960). Closing statement: Linguistics and poetics. In T. Sebeok (Ed.), *Style in language* (pp. 350–377). Cambridge, MA: MIT Press.

Jeon, M. (2001). Avoiding FOBs: An account of a journey. *Working Papers in Educational Linguistics, 17*(1/2), 83–106.

Kagiwada, G. (1989). The killing of Thong Ky Huynh: Implications of a Rashomon perspective. In G. Nomura, R. Endo, S. Sumida, & R. Leong (Eds.), *Frontiers of Asian American studies* (pp. 253–265). Pullman: Washington State University Press.

Kang, M. A. (2004). Constructing ethnic identity through discourse: Self-categorization among Korean American camp counselors. *Pragmatics, 14*(2/3), 217–233.

Kang, M. A., & Lo, A. (2004). Two ways of articulating heterogeneity in Korean American narratives of ethnic identity. *Journal of Asian American Studies, 7*(2), 93–116.

Katz, D., & Bradley, K. (1933). Racial stereotypes of one hundred students. *Journal of Abnormal and Social Psychology, 28,* 280–290.

Kennedy, R. L. (2002). *Nigger: The strange career of a troublesome word.* New York: Pantheon Books.

Kiang, P. N. (1996). *We could shape it: Organizing for Asian Pacific American student empowerment.* Boston: University of Massachusetts.

Kiang, P. N., & Kaplan, J. (1994). Where do we stand? Views of racial conflict by Vietnamese American high-school students in a black-and-white context. *The Urban Review, 26*(2), 95–119.

Kiang, P. N., Nguyen, N., & Sheehan, R. (1995). Don't ignore it: Documenting racial harassment in a fourth grade Vietnamese bilingual classroom. *Equity and Excellence in Education, 28*(1), 31–35.

Klein, W. (2005). *Turban narratives: Discourses of identity, visibility, and difference among Punjabi Sikh families in Los Angeles.* Unpublished manuscript.

Knox, G. (1992). *Gangs and related problems among Asian students: Preliminary findings from the first national Asian gang survey.* Unpublished manuscript.

Kochman, T. (1981). *Black and white styles in conflict.* Chicago: University of Chicago Press.

Koster, H. (Director). (1961). *Flower drum song* [Motion picture]. Universal City, CA: Universal International Pictures.

Kroskrity, P. (1993). Aspects of syntactic and semantic variation within the Arizona Tewa speech community. *Anthropological Linguistics, 35*(1–4), 250–273.

Labov, W. (1972). *Language in the inner city: Studies in Black English Vernacular.* Philadelphia: University of Pennsylvania Press.

Labov, W. (1980). Is there a creole speech community? In A. Valdman & A. Highfield (Eds.), *Theoretical orientations in Creole studies* (pp. 369–388). New York: Academic Press.

Le Page, R. B., & Tabouret-Keller, A. (1985). *Acts of identity: Creole-based approaches to language and ethnicity*. Cambridge, UK: Cambridge University Press.

Lee, A. (Director). (2002). *Crouching tiger, hidden dragon* [Motion picture]. Culver City, CA: Sony Pictures Classics.

Lee, R. (1999). *Orientals: Asian Americans in popular culture*. Philadelphia: Temple University Press.

Lee, S. (1996). *Unraveling the "model minority" stereotype: Listening to Asian American youth*. New York: Teachers College Press.

Lee, S. (2001). More than "model minorities" or "delinquents": A look at Hmong American high school students. *Harvard Educational Review, 71*(3), 505–528.

Leiner, D. (Director). (2004). *Harold and Kumar go to White Castle* [Motion picture]. Hollywood, CA: New Line Cinema.

Leyens, J., Yzerbyt, V., & Schadron, G. (1994). *Stereotypes and social cognition*. London: Sage.

Lim, J. H. (2001, June 22–28). Backstage with Gedde Watanabe. *AsianWeek*. Retrieved March 18, 2005, from http://www.asianweek.com/2001_06_22/ae1_geddewatanabe.html

Lin, J. (Director). (2002). *Better luck tomorrow* [Motion picture]. Hollywood, CA: Paramount Pictures.

Lippi-Green, R. (1997). *English with an accent: Language, ideology, and discrimination in the United States*. London: Routledge.

Lippmann, W. (1922). *Public opinion*. New York: Harcourt Brace.

Lo, A. (1999). Codeswitching, speech community membership, and the construction of ethnic identity. *Journal of Sociolinguistics, 3*(4), 461–479.

Lo, A., & Reyes, A. (Eds.). (2004). Relationality: Discursive constructions of Asian Pacific American identities. *Pragmatics, 14*(2/3).

Logan, J. (Director). (1957). *Sayonara* [Motion picture]. Hollywood, CA: William Goetz Productions.

Lopez, D., & Espiritu, Y. L. (1990). Panethnicity in the United States: A theoretical framework. *Ethnic and Racial Studies, 13*, 198–224.

Lowe, L. (1996). *Immigrant acts: On Asian American cultural politics*. Durham, NC: Duke University Press.

Lowry, I. S. (1982). The science and politics of ethnic enumeration. In W. A. Van Horne (Ed.), *Ethnicity and public policy* (Vol. 1, pp. 42–61). Madison: University of Wisconsin System.

Lyons, J. (1977). *Semantics*. Cambridge, UK: Cambridge University Press.

Maass, A., & Arcuri, L. (1992). The role of language in the persistence of stereotypes. In K. Fiedler & G. R. Semin (Eds.), *Language, interaction and social cognition* (pp. 129–143). Newbury Park, CA: Sage.

Marchetti, G. (1993). *Romance and the "yellow peril": Race, sex, and discursive strategies in Hollywood fiction.* Berkeley: University of California Press.

McLaren, P. (1997). *Revolutionary multiculturalism.* Boulder, CA: Westview.

Mendoza-Denton, N. (1996). "Muy macha": Gender and ideology in gang-girls' discourse about makeup. *Ethnos, 61*(1–2), 47–63.

Mendoza-Denton, N., & Iwai, M. (1993). "They speak more Caucasian": Generational differences in the speech of Japanese-Americans. In R. Queen & R. Barrett (Eds.), *SALSA I: Proceedings of the First Annual Symposium About Language and Society–Austin.* Austin: Department of Linguistics, University of Texas.

Metcalf, A. (1979). *Chicano English.* Arlington, VA: Center for Applied Linguistics.

Mitchell-Kernan, C. (1972). Signifying, loud-talking and marking. In T. Kochman (Ed.), *Rappin' and stylin' out: Communication in urban Black America* (pp. 315–335). Urbana: University of Illinois Press.

Morgan, M. (2001). Twisted in the anti-circle: Response to Mary Bucholtz, Word up: Social meanings of slang in California youth culture. *Language and Culture Online Symposium, 8.*

Moy, J. (1992). The death of Asia on the American field of representation. In S. Geor-Lim & A. Ling (Eds.), *Reading the literatures of Asian America* (pp. 349–357). Philadelphia: Temple University Press.

Mufwene, S. S., Rickford, J. R., Bailey, G., & Baugh, J. (Eds.). (1998). *African American English: Structure, history and use.* New York: Routledge.

Nagel, J. (1982). The political mobilization of Native Americans. *Social Science Journal, 19,* 37–45.

Nakanishi, D., & Hirano-Nakanishi, M. J. (Eds.). (1983). *The education of Asian Americans: Historical perspectives and prescriptions for the future.* Phoenix, AZ: Oryx Press.

Niedzwiecki, M., & Duong, T. C. (2004). *Southeast Asian American statistical profile.* Washington, DC: Southeast Asia Resource Action Center (SEARAC).

Ochs, E. (1990). Indexicality and socialization. In J. W. Stigler, R. A. Shweder, & G. Herdt (Eds.), *Cultural psychology: Essays on comparative human development* (pp. 287–308). Cambridge, UK: Cambridge University Press.

O'Connor, P. (1994). "You could feel it through the skin": Agency and positioning in prisoners' stabbing stories. *Text, 14*(1), 45–75.

Ogbu, J. (1974). *The next generation: An ethnography of education in an urban neighborhood.* New York: Academic Press.

Ogbu, J. (1977) Racial stratification and education: The case of Stockton, California. *ICRD Bulletin, 12*(3), 1–26.

Ogbu, J. (1978). *Minority education and caste: The American system in cross-cultural perspective.* New York: Academic Press.

Omi, M., & Winant, H. (1994). *Racial formation in the United States: From the 1960s to the 1990s.* New York: Routledge.

Padilla, F. M. (1985). *Latin ethnic consciousness: The case of Mexican Americans and Puerto Ricans in Chicago.* South Bend, IN: University of Notre Dame Press.

Peirce, C. (1932). *Collected papers of Charles Sanders Peirce, Vol. 2.* Cambridge, MA: Harvard University Press.

Peñalosa, F. (1980). *Chicano sociolinguistics: A brief introduction.* Rowley, MA: Newbury House.

Penfield, J., & Ornstein-Galicia, J. (1985). *Chicano English: An ethnic contact dialect.* Amsterdam: John Benjamins.

Peters, H. A. (1988). *A study of Southeast Asian youth in Philadelphia: A final report.* Washington, DC: Educational Resource Information Center.

Petitpas, A., & Champagne, D. (2000). Sports and social competence. In S. Danish & T. Gullotta (Eds.), *Developing competent youth and strong communities through after-school programming* (pp. 115–138). Washington, DC: Child Welfare League of America Press.

Philips, S. (1972). Participant structures and communicative competence: Warm Springs children in community and classroom. In C. Cazden, J. Vera, & D. Hymes (Eds.), *Function of language in the classroom* (pp. 370–394). New York: Teachers College Press.

Portes, A. (Ed.). (1996). *The new second generation.* New York: Russell Sage Foundation.

Portes, A., & Zhou, M. (1993). The new second generation: Segmented assimilation and its variants. *The Annals of the American Academy of Political and Social Sciences, 530,* 74–96.

Prashad, V. (2002). *Everybody was kung fu fighting: Afro-Asian connections and the myth of cultural purity.* Boston: Beacon Press.

Putnam, H. (1975). *Mind, language and reality.* London: Cambridge University Press.

Rampton, B. (1995a). *Crossing: Language and ethnicity among adolescents.* London: Longman.

Rampton, B. (1995b). Language crossing and the problematisation of ethnicity and socialization. *Pragmatics, 5,* 485–513.

Rampton, B. (1999). Styling the other: Introduction. *Journal of Sociolinguistics, 3*(4), 421–427.

Reeves, T. J., & Bennett, C. E. (2004). *We the people: Asians in the United States* (Census 2000 Special Reports, CENSR-17). Washington, DC: U.S. Census Bureau.

Reyes, A. (2002). "Are you losing your culture?" Poetics, indexicality and Asian American identity. *Discourse Studies, 4*(2), 183–199.

Reyes, A. (2004). Asian American stereotypes as circulating resource. *Pragmatics, 14*(2/3), 173–192.

Reyes, A., & Lo, A. (2004). Language, identity and relationality: An introduction. *Pragmatics, 14*(2/3), 115–125.

Rickford, J. R. (1996). Regional and social variation. In S. McKay & N. H. Hornberger (Eds.), *Sociolinguistics and language teaching* (pp. 151–194). New York: Cambridge University Press.

Rickford, J. R., & Rickford, R. J. (2000). *Spoken soul: The story of Black English.* New York: Wiley.

Ronkin, M., & Karn, H. (1999). Mock Ebonics: Linguistic racism in parodies of Ebonics on the Internet. *Journal of Sociolinguistics, 3*(3), 360–380.

Rumbaut, R. G., & Ima, K. (1988). *The adaptation of Southeast Asian refugee youth: A comparative study. Final report to the Office of Resettlement.* San Diego, CA: San Diego State University.

Ryan, E. (1979). Why do low-prestige language varieties persist? In H. Giles & R. N. St. Clair (Eds.), *Language and social psychology* (pp. 145–157). Oxford, UK: Blackwell.

Rymes, B. (1996). Rights to advise: Advice as an emergent phenomenon in student-teacher talk. *Linguistics and Education, 8*, 409–437.

Rymes, B. (2001). *Conversational borderlands: Language and identity in an alternative urban high school.* New York: Teachers College Press.

Said, E. (1978). *Orientalism.* New York: Pantheon Books.

Schiffrin, D. (1987). *Discourse markers.* New York: Cambridge University Press.

Semons, M. (1991). Ethnicity in the urban high school: A naturalistic study of student experiences. *The Urban Review, 23*(3), 137–158.

Sethi, R. (1994). Smells like racism: A plan for mobilizing against anti-Asian bias. In K. Aguilar-San Juan (Ed.), *The state of Asian America: Activism and resistance in the 1990s* (pp. 235–250). Boston: South End Press.

Shepperson, G. (1985). *A descriptive study of an after school sex education program for fifth and sixth grade students.* Unpublished doctoral dissertation, University of Pennsylvania, Philadelphia.

Silverstein, M. (1976). Shifters, linguistic categories, and cultural description. In K. Basso & H. Selby (Eds.), *Meaning in anthropology* (pp. 11–55). Albuquerque: University of New Mexico Press.

Silverstein, M. (1993). Metapragmatic discourse and metapragmatic function. In J. Lucy (Ed.), *Reflexive language: Reported speech and metapragmatics* (pp. 33–58). New York: Cambridge University Press.

Silverstein, M. (1998). The improvisational performance of culture in realtime discursive practice. In R. Sawyer (Ed.), *Creativity in performance* (pp. 265–312). Greenwich, CT: Ablex.

Silverstein, M., & Urban, G. (1996). The natural history of discourse. In M. Silverstein & G. Urban (Eds.), *Natural histories of discourse* (pp. 1–17). Chicago: University of Chicago Press.

Sledd, J. (1965). On not teaching English usage. *English Journal, 54*, 698–703.

Smitherman, G. (1977). *Talkin and testifyin: The language of Black America.* New York: Harper & Row.

Smitherman, G. (2000). *Black talk: Words and phrases from the hood to the amen corner.* Boston: Houghton Mifflin.

Soe, V. (Director). (1985). *All Orientals look the same* [Video]. San Francisco, CA: Center for Asian American Media.

Spencer, R. (1950). Japanese American language behavior. *American Speech, 25*(4), 241–252.

Spheeris, P. (Director). (1992). *Wayne's world* [Motion picture]. Hollywood, CA: Paramount Pictures.

Spurlock, M. (2004a). *Director's statement.* Retrieved June 2, 2005, from http://www.supersizeme.com/home.aspx?page=aboutdirector

Spurlock, M. (Director). (2004b). *Super size me* [Motion picture]. New York: The Con.

Stangor, C., & Schaller, M. (1996). Stereotypes as individual and collective representations. In C. Macrae, C. Stangor, & M. Hewstone (Eds.), *Stereotypes and stereotyping* (pp. 3–40). New York: Guildford Press.

Suárez-Orozco, M. (1991). Immigrant adaptation to schooling: A Hispanic case. In M. Gibson & J. Ogbu (Eds.), *Minority status and schooling: A comparative study of immigrant and involuntary minorities* (pp. 37–61). New York: Garland.

Sweetland, J. (2002). Unexpected but authentic use of an ethnically-marked dialect. *Journal of Sociolinguistics, 6*(4), 514–536.

Tajfel, H. (Ed.). (1978). *Differentiation between social groups: Studies in the social psychology of intergroup relations.* London: Academic Press

Tajfel, H. (1981). *Human groups and social categories.* Cambridge, UK: Cambridge University Press.

Takaki, R. (1989). *Strangers from a different shore: A history of Asian Americans.* Boston: Little, Brown.

Talmy, S. (2004). Forever fob: The cultural production of ESL in a high school. *Pragmatics, 14*(2/3), 149–172.

Tollefson, J. (1989). *Alien winds: The reeducation of America's Indochinese refugees.* New York: Praeger.

Tong, S. (Director). (1992). *Supercop* [Motion picture]. Hong Kong, China: Golden Harvest Company, Ltd.

Trueba, H., Cheng, L., & Ima, K. (1993). *Myth or reality: Adaptive strategies of Asian Americans in California.* Washington, DC: Falmer.

Tuan, M. (1998). *Forever foreigners or honorary whites? The Asian ethnic experience today.* New Brunswick, NJ: Rutgers University Press.

Turner, J. C. (1982). Towards a cognitive redefinition of the social group. In H. Tajfel (Ed.), *Social Identity and Intergroup relations* (pp. 15–40). Cambridge, UK: Cambridge University Press.

Urban, G. (2001). *Metaculture: How culture moves through the world.* Minneapolis: University of Minnesota Press.

van Dijk, T. (1987). *Communicating racism: Ethnic prejudice in thought and talk.* Newbury Park, CA: Sage.

Vigil, J., & Yun, S. (1990). Vietnamese youth gangs in Southern California. In R. Huff (Ed.), *Gangs in America: Diffusion, diversity, and public policy* (pp. 146–162). Beverly Hills, CA: Sage.

Wang, W. (Director). (1982). *Chan is missing* [Motion picture]. New York: New Yorker Films.

Wang, W. (Director). (1993). *Joy luck club* [Motion picture]. Hollywood, CA: Hollywood Pictures.

Waters, M. (1990). *Ethnic options: Choosing identities in America.* Berkeley: University of California Press.

Weis, L., & Fine, M. (Eds.). (2000). *Construction sites: Excavating race, class, gender and sexuality in spaces for and by youth.* New York: Teachers College Press.

Williams, R. (1976). *Keywords: A vocabulary of culture and society.* New York: Oxford University Press.

Wilson, C., & Gutierrez, F. (1985). *Minorities and the media: Diversity and the end of mass communication.* Newbury Park, CA: Sage.

Wolfram, W., Christian, D., & Hatfield, D. (1986). The English of adolescent and young adult Vietnamese refugees in the United States. *World Englishes, 5*(1), 47–60.

Woolard, K. A. (1985). Language variation and cultural hegemony: Toward an integration of sociolinguistic and social theory. *American Ethnologist, 12*(4), 738–748.

Wortham, S. (1994). *Acting out participant examples in the classroom.* Philadelphia: John Benjamins.

Wortham, S. (2001). *Narratives in action.* New York: Teachers College Press.

Wortham, S. (2003). Linguistic anthropology of education: An introduction. In S. Wortham & B. Rymes (Eds.), *Linguistic anthropology of education* (pp. 1–29). Westport, CT: Praeger.

Wortham, S., & Locher, M. (1996). Voicing on the news: An analytic technique for studying media bias. *Text, 16*(4), 557–585.

Wortham, S., & Rymes, B. (Eds.). (2003). *Linguistic anthropology of education.* Westport, CT: Praeger.

Xing, J. (1998). *Asian America through the lens: History, representations, and identity.* Walnut Creek, CA: Altamira Press.

Zuengler, J. (1989). Identity and IL development and use. *Applied Linguistics, 10*(1), 80–96.

Appendix

TRANSCRIPTION CONVENTIONS

Convention	Description
<u>word</u>	(underline) utterance stress
word?	(question mark) rising intonation
word.	(period) falling intonation
word,	(comma) falling-rising intonation
word-	(dash) abrupt breaks or stops
wo:rd	(colon) elongated vowel or consonant
word	(italics) non-English word
{word}	(curly braces around word) English translation
°word°	(circles around word) utterance is quieter than surrounding talk
wo(hh)rd	(hh) laughter breaking into utterance
(.)	(period in parentheses) a pause under 0.5
(0.5)	(number in parentheses) a silence measured 0.5 or more
(word)	(parentheses) doubtful transcription or conjecture
(?)	(question mark in parentheses) inaudible utterance
<word>	(arrows around word) transcriber comment
...	(ellipsis) deleted segment in transcript
[word [word	(brackets) simultaneous talk
word= =word	(equal sign) continuous talk

PHONETIC SYMBOLS

Symbol	Sample Words
[p]	pin, happy
[b]	bat, ribbon
[t]	tall, star
[d]	dog, sad
[k]	cat, basket
[g]	goat, lag
[ʔ]	(glottal stop) uh-oh, kitten
[f]	fit, laugh
[v]	vase, savvy
[θ]	think, bath
[ð]	the, bathe
[s]	sit, dice
[z]	zebra, resign
[ʃ]	shine, nation
[ʒ]	measure, beige
[h]	who, unhand
[tʃ]	child, catch
[dʒ]	jump, gadget
[m]	miss, calm
[n]	need, bin
[ŋ]	long, singer
[l]	list, fall
[ɹ]	(retroflex liquid) run, stir
[r]	(trilled "r") e.g., in Spanish: arroz, carro
[ɾ]	(alveolar flap) later, riddle
[w]	win, lower
[j]	yam, beauty
[ʰ]	(aspiration) e.g., [pʰ] in pin, but not spin
[i]	beat, merry

[ɪ]	b<u>i</u>t, <u>i</u>nto
[e]	b<u>ai</u>t, str<u>ay</u>
[ɛ]	b<u>e</u>t, g<u>ue</u>st
[æ]	b<u>a</u>t, l<u>au</u>gh
[u]	s<u>ui</u>t, l<u>o</u>se
[ʊ]	s<u>oo</u>t, p<u>u</u>ll
[o]	c<u>oa</u>t, l<u>ow</u>
[ɔ]	c<u>au</u>ght, l<u>aw</u>
[a]	c<u>o</u>t, f<u>a</u>ther
[ʌ]	c<u>u</u>t, tr<u>ou</u>ble
[ə]	<u>a</u>mong, sof<u>a</u>
[aɪ]	<u>ai</u>sle, s<u>igh</u>
[aʊ]	<u>ow</u>l, l<u>ou</u>d
[ɔɪ]	<u>oi</u>l, s<u>oy</u>

Author Index

A

Agha, A., 6, 37, 70, 113, 118
Arcuri, L., 6

B

Badey, J., 12, 151
Bailey, B., 5, 28, 92
Bailey, G., 65
Bakhtin, M., 54, 67, 132, 139
Ball, A., 153
Bancroft, T., 40
Barnes, J. S., 118
Barth, F., 92
Baugh, J., 65
Bauman, R., 6, 118
Bennett, C. E., 8, 118
Beebe, L., 64
Bell, A., 37, 70
Benveniste, E., 42, 71, 132
Bourdieu, P., 78
Bourhis, R. Y., 17
Bradley, K., 6
Briggs, C., 6, 118
Bucholtz, M., 5, 15, 28, 44, 66, 67, 68,
        69, 70, 81, 82
Burks, A., 42

C

Champagne, D., 153
Chan, K., 11, 150
Chapman, R. L., 68
Chin, K., 12, 151
Cheng, L., 11, 150
Choy, C., 155
Christian, D., 66
Chun, E., x, 29, 34, 37, 38, 39, 45, 67,
        75, 110
Cook, B., 40
Coupland, N., 37, 70
Cutler, C. A., 67

D

Duranti, A., 117
De Mille, C. B., 8
Duong, T. C., 13, 14, 23, 118

E

Eble, C., 35, 68, 69, 70, 72
Eccles, J., 151
Eckert, P., 37, 70, 78
Eisenstein, M., 64
Ellis, R., 64
Espiritu, Y. L., 3, 4, 26, 93, 114

F

Fine, M., 15, 151
Foley, D. E., 17
Fong, T., 8
Fought, C., 66
Fung, R., 154

G

Gal, S., 7, 37, 54
Gergen, K., 106
Gibson, M., 10
Giles, H., 17
Goffman, E., 67, 112, 118, 123, 141
Goldstein, L., 64
Goodwin, C., 108, 109
Goodwin, M., 5, 28, 108
Gootman, J., 151
Green, L., 68
Griffith, D. W., 8
Gullotta, C., 153, 154
Gutierrez, F., 6

H

Habermas, J., 154
Hagedorn, J., 8
Hall, K., 5, 44, 67
Hall, S., 17, 28, 92
Halliday, M. A. K., 69
Hamamoto, D., 8, 28
Hamovitch, B., 153
Hanna, D. B., 66
Hatala, E., 67
Hatfield, D., 66
He, A., 29
Heath, S. B., 28, 29, 79, 151, 153, 154
Hebdige, D., 154

Heller, M., 136, 137
Hewitt, R., 66, 67, 68
Hill, J., 37, 75
Hirano-Nakanishi, M. J., 11, 150
Hughes, J., 40
Hull, G., 151
Hune, S., 11, 150
Hymes, D., 29

I

Ima, K., 11, 24, 150
Irby, M., 151
Irvine, J., 7, 37, 53, 70
Iwai, M., 66

J

Jagose, A., 122
Jakobson, R., 44
Jeon, M., 32, 35, 36

K

Kagiwada, G., 150
Kang, M. A., 32, 93
Kaplan, J., 150
Karn, H., 37, 38, 75
Katz, D., 6
Kaye, J., 106
Kennedy, R. L., 121, 122
Kiang, P. N., 11, 150
Klein, W., 150
Knox, G., 151
Kochman, T., 65
Koster, H., 156
Kroskrity, P., 5

L

Labov, W., 65, 67
Le Page, R. B., 66, 76, 91
Lee, A., 95
Lee, R., 8, 10, 28
Lee, S., 10, 11, 15, 17, 21, 28, 124, 150
Leiner, D., 157
Leyens, J., 6, 7
Lim, J. H., 41
Lin, J., 157
Lippi-Green, R., 37
Lippmann, W., 6
Lo, A., 29, 32, 66, 67
Locher, M., 104
Logan, J., 8
Lopez, D., 3
Lowe, L., 3, 4, 8, 121, 136
Lowry, I. S., 3
Lyons, J., 43

M

Maass, A., 6
Marchetti, G., 8, 28
McLaren, P., 142
McLaughlin, M. W., 79, 151
Mendoza-Denton, N., 66, 93
Metcalf, A., 66
Mitchell-Kernan, C., 65
Morgan, M., 76
Moy, J., 8
Mufwene, S., 65

N

Nagel, J., 93
Nakanishi, D., 11, 150
Nguyen, N., 150

Niedzwiecki, M., 13, 14, 23, 118

O

Ochs, E., 38, 75
O'Connor, P., 43
Ogbu, J., 10, 11
Omi, M., 92
Ornstein-Galicia, J., 66

P

Padilla, F. M., 93
Peirce, C., 42, 71, 132
Peñalosa, F., 66
Penfield, J., 66
Peters, H. A., 12
Petitpas, A., 153
Philips, S., 29
Plant, R., 153, 154
Portes, A., 24, 62, 63
Prashad, V., 63, 99, 142
Putnam, H., 16, 104, 119

R

Rampton, B., 5, 28, 34, 37, 38, 40, 63, 66, 67, 68, 75, 92
Reeves, T. J., 8
Reyes, A., 29, 64, 66, 67
Rickford, J. R., 36, 37, 65, 70
Rickford, R. J., 65
Ronkin, M., 37, 38, 75
Rumbaut, R. G., 24
Ryan, E., 66
Rymes, B., 5, 28, 29, 152

S

Said, E., 8, 42
Schadron, G., 6, 7
Schaller, M., 6
Schiffrin, D., 72
Schultz, K., 151
Semons, M., 150
Sethi, R., 99
Sheehan, R., 150
Shepperson, G., 153
Silverstein, M., 6, 42, 70, 71, 84, 105,
        106, 117, 118, 131, 132
Sledd, J., 69
Smitherman, G., 65, 75
Soe, V., 155
Spencer, R., 66
Spheeris, P., 40
Spurlock, M., 154
Stangor, C., 6
Suárez-Orozco, M., 10
Sweetland, J., 67, 68, 86

T

Tabouret-Keller, A., 66, 76, 91
Tajfel, H., 17,
Tajima, R., 155
Takaki, R., 8, 9, 11, 118
Talmy, S., 32, 35
Taylor, D. M., 17
Tollefson, J., 23
Tong, S., 40
Trueba, H., 11, 150
Tuan, M., 7, 10, 15
Turner, J. C., 17

U

Urban, G., 6, 117, 118

V

van Dijk, T., 75
Vigil, J., 12, 151

W

Wang, W., 155, 156
Waters, M., 92
Weis, L., 151
Williams, R., 117
Wilson, C., 6
Winant, H., 92
Wolfram, W., 66
Woolard, K. A., 78
Wortham, S., 28, 29, 104, 106

X

Xing, J., 154, 155

Y

Yun, S., 12, 151
Yzerbyt, V., 6, 7

Z

Zhou, M., 62, 63
Zuengler, J., 64

Subject Index

1.5 generation, *see also* Generation, 24,
 32–33, 36, 51, 58–59, 116,
 126, 136
249, see also Videos, 30, 50–51, 155

A

Accent, *see also* F.O.B., Mock Asian,
 x, 8, 33–34, 36–37, 41, 46,
 48, 63
African Americans, ix–x, 3, 7, 9–16,
 24, 31, 38, 54, 62–65, 67–69,
 72–78, 81–82, 86–88, 92, 99,
 116, 122, 127, 138–139, 141,
 145, 148–150
African American Vernacular English
 (AAVE), 38, 42, 51, 54, 56,
 58, 63–68, 75–76, 81, 139
After-school education, *see also* Asian
 Americans, Media, 21–23,
 150–153
American Sroksrei, *see also* Videos,
 29–30, 77, 116, 131, 146, 155
Asian American identity, *see* Identity
Asian Americans, *see also* East Asian
 Americans, Southeast Asian
 Americans, ix, 1–5, 7–15, 17,
 29, 38, 69, 76, 87, 93, 99,
 121, 136
 and discrimination, *see also* Ethnic epithet, 3, 8–9, 23,
 35–36, 76, 150, 154–155
 and education, *see also* After-
 school education, 10–15,
 17, 21, 28–29, 32, 78,
 150–153
 and gangs, 2, 12, 15, 21–24,
 29–30, 78, 116, 151–153
 and language, 27–29, 66–69,
 148–149
 and media, *see also* Media, 3–4,
 8–10, 27, 40, 44–45,
 50–51, 58–61, 99, 102,
 105, 118, 120, 130, 141,
 150, 154–157
Assimilation, segmented, 62–63
Authentication, 34, 44–45, 47–48,
 50–51, 59–60, 65–67, 78–79,
 82, 84, 86–88

B

Ba. Bay. Three., *see also* Videos, 30,
 50–51, 52–59, 61, 79, 102,
 130, 155

C

Chink, *see also* Ethnic epithet, 121
 as insult term, 48, 121–122
 reappropriation of, 27, 122–123
Circulation, 6–7, 112–113, 117–120,
 141–144

Crouching Tiger, Hidden Dragon,
        95–96
Culture, 117–118, 142–143
        caught between two, 116, 134
        as emblem of ethnic differentia-
                tion, 137–142
        as historical transmission,
                132–137
        loss of, 116, 135–136, 137–138,
                142–143

        D

Denotational text, 84–86, 106, 131

        E

East Asian Americans, 2, 4, 9, 11,
        13–15, 35–36, 75–76, 90, 93,
        99, 115, 117–118, 120–122,
        124–126, 138–143, 151, 155
Ebonics, *see also* African American
        Vernacular English, 37–38,
        68
Education, *see* After-school education,
        Asian Americans, Media
ESL (English as a second language),
        32, 64
Ethnic epithet, *see also* Chink, F.O.B.,
        Gook, 121–123
Ethnic identity, *see* Identity
Ethnicity, ix, 91–93, 113, 115,
        117–120, 125–126, 139,
        142–143, 149
        interethnic issues, 30, 52, 63, 102,
                124, 126–130, 152
        multiethnic issues, 25, 62, 114,
                125

Ethnic kind, 119–120, 122–123, 126,
        128, 130, 139, 143
Ethnic pride, 123–126, 143, 153
European Americans, *see also* Man,
        the, 7–15, 17, 26, 31–32,
        34–35, 38, 41–42, 44–46,
        49–50, 60, 62, 67–69, 72,
        75–76, 81, 86, 116, 141, 155

        F

Family, 2, 16, 23, 25, 30, 33–36,
        44–46, 49, 51, 54–56, 58–60,
        100–101, 103, 106–109,
        111–112, 116, 128–130,
        132–136, 138–139, 141, 146
First generation, *see also* Generation,
        32–36, 51, 58–60, 125–126,
        136
F.O.B. (Fresh Off the Boat), *see also*
        Ethnic epithet, Forever for-
        eigner, x, 31–33, 35–36, 51,
        126
        and accent, *see also* Accent, Mock
                Asian, 33–34, 36–37
        and unacculturation, 35–37, 51,
                59–60
        and xenophobia, 35–37
Forever foreigner, *see also* F.O.B., x,
        7–9, 11–12, 15, 26, 32,
        34–36, 38–39, 45–46, 50–51,
        54, 59–61, 69, 87, 114, 133,
        136, 148–149, 155

        G

Gang, *see* Asian Americans
Generation, *see also* 1.5 generation,
        First generation, Second gen-

eration, 30, 51, 117, 125–126, 129–130, 136, 143, 152
Ghetto, 68, 73–74, 77–78
Gook, *see also* Ethnic epithet, 48, 121–124

H

Hip hop, 24, 30, 54, 62–63, 77, 116, 145–146
Honorary White, *see also* Model minority, 7, 9–12, 15, 25, 38, 69, 87, 99, 150

I

Identity, ix, 4–5, 16–17, 27–29, 66–67, 76, 82, 92–93, 106–107, 136, 142–143, 147–149, 151–153
Asian American identity, 1–5, 34, 36, 49, 51, 56, 58, 60–63, 66, 76–77, 87, 90, 112–114, 123, 148–149, 152–153
ethnic identity, 92–93, 121, 123
and labels, 2, 5, 31–32, 90
politics of, 136-137, 142
Indexicality, 37, 42–43, 51, 70–71, 86–87, 104–105, 131–132, 136, 139, 141–142, 149
dual indexicality, 38, 74–75
and pronouns, 43–50, 71, 81–82, 132
triple indexicality, 75–78
Interactional text, 84, 106, 131, 141

L

Language crossing, 37–38, 66, 75
Latino Americans, ix, 3, 10, 12, 28, 64, 66, 92–93
Linguistic capital, 78
Long Duk Dong, *see also Sixteen Candles*, 40–42, 44, 46–48, 59

M

Mainstream American English (MAE), 38, 41, 51–52, 54, 56–58, 72, 80
Man, the, *see also* European Americans, 43–46, 49–51, 59–60
Media, 6–7, 154, 156
and Asian Americans, *see* Asian Americans
and education, *see also* After-school education, 21–23, 153–157
Metapragmatics, 70, 74, 76, 84–85, 105–106, 138
Mock Asian, 34–42, 44–58, 60, 149
Model minority, *see also* Honorary White, 10, 12–15, 17, 25, 99, 114, 150–151, 155
Multiculturalism, 118, 141-142

O

Other Asian, *see also* Southeast Asian Americans, ix, 1, 3–5, 11, 14–16, 26, 76–77, 87, 90–91, 114–117, 130, 141, 144–145, 147–149, 153

P

Panethnicity, ix–xi, 3–4, 89–91, 93,
        96–100, 109–111, 113–117,
        119, 121–124, 126–127,
        129–130, 141–144, 149, 153
Participants, 23–27
        Anh, 25, 51–52, 56–57, 62, 72–75,
              82–87, 100–101,
              107–113, 121–122
        Chea, 40, 83, 85–86, 94–95, 122
        Enoy, 33, 79–80, 102–112, 115,
              124, 127–129
        Moeun, 25, 32–34, 47–48, 50–51,
              62, 100–101, 104–112,
              121–122, 131, 133–135,
              137–140, 145–147, 156
        Sokla, 1–5, 11, 18–20, 46–48, 50,
              72, 76–78, 87, 89–91,
              93, 116, 145, 147–148,
              155–156
        Van, 73–75, 78, 81, 83–84, 87,
              94–99, 111, 113, 149
Problem minority, x, 12–16, 25, 38, 65,
        69, 87, 148, 151
Pronouns, *see* Indexicality

R

Race, ix–x, 3–4, 7–15, 32, 66, 69, 72,
        75, 81, 85–87, 91–93, 96,
        113, 121, 127, 139, 141–142,
        149–150
Racialization, 4, 38, 65–68, 73–79,
        87–88
Recursivity, 54
Refugee, 2–3, 12, 23–24, 133
Research process, 18–30

S

Second generation, *see also* Genera-
        tion, 24, 32–33, 36, 51,
        58–59, 116, 126, 136
Sixteen Candles, see also Long Duk
        Dong, 40, 43–44, 60–61
Slang, x, 54, 65, 68–88, 149, 153, 156
Southeast Asian Americans, *see also*
        Other Asian, ix, 2, 11–16,
        23–27, 29–30, 69, 76, 78, 87,
        90, 109, 115–116, 119–120,
        122, 124, 141, 143, 148,
        151–153
Speech chain, 6–7, 113, 118, 120, 143
Stereotypes, *see also* Forever foreigner,
        Honorary White, Model mi-
        nority, Problem minority,
        Typification, 6, 16–17,
        27–28, 31, 91, 104–107, 110,
        119, 148–149, 157
    all Asians look alike, 117,
              120–122, 130, 139, 141,
              143, 155
    anthropological perspectives on,
              ix, 6–7, 17, 28
    Asian American studies perspec-
              tives on, 7, 27–28
    food, 96–99, 113
    inhabiting of, 94–96, 101,
              106–109, 149
    martial arts, 8, 16, 39–40, 63,
              94–96, 113, 149
    minivan driver, 101, 105, 108–113
    as oppressive, 32, 36, 38, 40,
              43–46, 50, 75, 94, 99,
              101, 107, 109–110,
              121–123, 125, 144,
              149–151, 154–155
    as resource, 28, 34, 40, 75, 87, 91,
              93–97, 107–108,

110–111, 113–114,
122–123, 144, 148–149,
157
social psychological perspectives
on, ix, 6–7, 17
storeowner, 16, 99–113, 156
Style, x, 32, 34–38, 51, 53–54, 56–57,
65–67, 69–70, 81, 156

T

These Are the Days, see also Videos,
30, 83, 94, 155
Typification, 6, 108, 111
local typification, 100, 105–106,
109, 111–113
widespread typification, *see also*
Stereotypes, 16, 100,
105–106, 111, 149

V

Videos, *see 249, American Sroksrei,
Ba. Bay. Three., These Are
the Days*
Voicing, 54, 67, 139–141